ISBN 978-1-332-89427-7
PIBN 10433947

OUR HERO

GENERAL U. S. GRANT.

WHEN, WHERE,
AND
HOW HE FOUGHT.

IN WORDS OF ONE SYLLABLE,

BY
JOSEPHINE POLLARD.

WITH
EIGHTY-SIX ETCHINGS,
BY EDWIN FORBES

NEW YORK:
McLOUGHLIN BROTHERS, PUBLISHERS.

A WORD TO THE SMALL BOY.

This is a book for boys;—small boys, from six to twelve years of age, who love to read, or to be read to, from books that are not chock full of great big words. It is not a book for girls at all. They will not care for it. The big boy, who does not have to stop to spell out the long words and guess what they mean, will turn up his nose at it. But let him. That will not hurt us. It is the small boy we have set out to please, and if he reads what is here told of U. S. Grant he will—when he grows up—seek to know more of this great and good man, to whom we, of the U-nited States, owe so much.

If this book should teach the least one of the small boys to fear God—to do right—to speak the truth—to love peace—and to be brave and true through and through—it will have done all and more than was hoped for by

THE AUTHOR.

CONTENTS

CHAPTER I.	AS A BOY	5
CHAPTER II.	AT WEST POINT	9
CHAPTER III.	ON THE WAR PATH	14
CHAPTER IV.	FORT HENRY AND FORT DONELSON	21
CHAPTER V.	TWO DAYS OF BLOOD	30
CHAPTER VI.	THE SIEGE OF CORINTH	38
CHAPTER VII.	THE SIEGE OF VICKSBURG	44
CHAPTER VIII.	AT CHATTANOOGA	58
CHAPTER IX.	THE BATTLE OF THE WILDERNESS	70
CHAPTER X.	BY THE LEFT FLANK	78
CHAPTER XI.	THE SIEGE OF PETERSBURG	92
CHAPTER XII.	THE MARCH TO THE SEA	111
CHAPTER XIII.	THE FIGHT AT CEDAR CREEK	119
CHAPTER XIV.	THE FIGHT AT FIVE FORKS	128
CHAPTER XV.	ON TO RICHMOND	144
CHAPTER XVI.	"LET US HAVE PEACE"	152
CHAPTER XVII.	THE LAST FIGHT OF ALL	164

FULL PAGE ILLUSTRATIONS.

GENERAL GRANT ON THE WAY TO CITY POINT AFTER THE SURRENDER OF LEE.

II. BATTLE OF BELMONT.

III. THE ATTACK ON FORT DONELSON.

IV. BATTLE OF SHILOH.

V. BATTLE OF CHAMPION'S HILL.

VI. THE SIEGE OF VICKSBURG. THE CRATER.

VII. BATTLE AMONG THE CLOUDS—LOOKOUT MOUNTAIN.

VIII. BATTLE OF THE WILDERNESS.

IX. BATTLE OF SPOTTSYLVANIA COURT-HOUSE.

X. CHARGE AT COLD HARBOR.

XI. CHARGE ON THE EXPLODED MINE AT PETERSBURG.

XII. THE CAVALRY CHARGE AT FISHER'S HILL.

XIII. THE REBEL ARMY RETREATING FROM RICHMOND.

XIV. THE MEETING OF GENERALS GRANT AND LEE.

XV. GENERAL LEE'S ARMY AFTER THE SURRENDER.

OUR HERO
GENERAL U. S. GRANT.

CHAPTER I.

AS A BOY.

WE all like to read, or to hear, of the great men of the age, to know how and where they lived, what kind of boys they were, and how they rose to their high place, and won their fame.

U-lys-ses S. Grant was a poor boy. He was born at Point Pleas-ant, O-hi-o, on the 27th day of A-pril, 1822. He was not as bright and smart as some boys are, but was thought to be quite dull and slow at school, and more fond of a horse than he was of a book. If there was a wild rough horse that no one would dare to mount, U-lys-ses would leap on its back and ride off with no thought of fear.

A man whose farm was not far from the Grants, had a horse that he could not train. He had seen U-lys-ses break in more than one wild colt, and he thought it would be a good plan to get him to try his hand on this one. But U-lys-ses was too proud to do this kind of work for hire. The man knew that; so he came up one day as if in great haste, and said to the ten year old boy, "I wish you would take this note from me to a man in the next town. I have no time to go, as there is work to be done on the farm, but if you will go I will pay you well. My horse is swift, and will take you there and bring you back in no time."

U-lys-ses said "I will go." He was in need of cash, and this was a good chance to earn some. So up he got on the horse, took the reins in his hands, and just as he set off the man cried out to him, as if he had just thought of it, when it had been on his mind all the while—"I want you to teach that horse how to pace."

BREAK-ING THE HORSE.

It was a hard task and U-lys-ses had a fight with the horse all the way to town and part of the way back. At last the horse gave in and made up his mind to change his gait to please the small boy on his back, who stuck like a bur, and was not to be thrown off, though the horse tried his best to get rid of him.

Of course, the man who owned the horse was much pleased, but it was not long ere U-lys-ses found out that the whole thing was a trick to get him to break in the horse, and he did not like it at all. He thought the man should have told him the truth, for a boy who is fond of the truth does not like to have a lie told, or to be made a fool or a tool of in this way. Though he was well paid for what he did, he made up his mind that he would do no more of that kind of work, which was much too low to suit his taste.

U-lys-ses was quite small for his age, but did not like to drive the small team in use on the farm. He was fond of a big horse, and when Dan was bought as a mate to the one on the place, U-lys-ses was in high glee. When eight years old he could hitch up the team and drive off as well as a man, and when twelve years old would haul great logs and load up the cart with no one to help him but Dan.

The boy would fix a chain round a log and get Dan to pull it up near the cart, and with a haul here and a pull there would work it in place, and think it no great thing to do.

The boy, you see, had a wise head, and knew how to plan his work, and how to pull through a tight place, and these traits grew strong day by day and made him the brave calm man he grew to be.

But I must tell you how he came to be known as U-lys-ses S. Grant, when that was not his right name at all. His real name was Hi-ram U-lys-ses, but when the boys at school gave him the nick-name of "Hug", he thought it was time to change it. So he wrote his name U-lys-ses H. Grant.

A friend who had a chance to send a boy to West Point, thought that U-lys-ses would be glad to go and would be the right boy for the place. He knew that one of the Grant boys had Simp-son as part of his name, and so he wrote to West Point that the boy he sent bore the name of U-lys-ses Simp-son Grant, and when Grant found this out he let it go. It was a good thing, and, I have no doubt, part of a wise plan, for these things do not take place by chance. H. U. Grant, or U. H. Grant, would not have been so strong as U. S. Grant, which seems to bring him near to us and to the land for which he fought.

Most of those who go to West Point have a taste for war, but Grant was more fond of peace, and did not care to go to this kind of a school. But it was thought best that he should. The young men there soon gave him the nick-name of "Un-cle Sam," and this stuck to him all through the rest of his life.

CHAPTER II.

AT WEST POINT.

It was in the year 1839 that Grant went to West Point, and not much is told of his life at that place. West Point is a school where the drill is the same year in and year out, and where young men are sent from all parts of the U-ni-ted States, to learn the art of war.

U-lys-ses did not need to be taught, as some of the boys did, how to mount or to ride a horse. He knew all that. He made friends while there who were warm friends till the day of his death, who knew that he tried to do what was right, was just, and true, and had a clean head and a pure mind. He did not talk much, but was as fond of fun as most boys are. But it had to be the right kind of fun or he would take

GRANT AS A CA-DET.

no part in it. He did not swear, and had no taste for coarse jokes; which is more than can be said of most men. Boys are apt to think it a fine thing to swear; and men laugh when they hear them speak "the big round oath," which they so soon learn to use in their talk, and find so hard to get rid of.

This one thing shows how brave Grant was at this time, and how firm to stick to what he thought was the right course. He had set out to be a good man, and a clean man, and God gave him strength to turn from all that was bad, and to live so that he would not have to blush with shame for his past deeds. He could not have known then how high he was to stand in the eyes of the world, how each act of his life would be brought out and held up to view in the clear light of fame.

No boy knows just where he will stand when he is a man. He may plot and plan all his young days, and try his best to win the prize of fame, but all his plans may fall through, all his deep laid schemes may come to nought. Those who lead the race for a while may not have the luck to reach the goal. The best way is to do right all the time, and to live so as to gain a good name, and to be known as a good man, if it is not your fate to be known as a great one.

Grant stood well in his class at West Point, and at the end of the four years' course was sent to join the troops with Gen-er-al Zach-a-ry Tay-lor, who was then in Tex-as. This was in the year 1843.

War with Mex-i-co broke out in 1846, and Grant took part in the fight at Pa-lo Al'-to, Re-sa-ca de la Pal-ma, Cer-ro Gor-do, Chur-u-bus-co, Mo-li-no del Rey, and Cha-pul-te-pec, and went on with the troops that fought their way to the Cit-y of Mex-i-co, which they took by storm, in the year 1847.

I hope you have a map to look at as you read these queer names, and will trace out the route the troops took in their march from the camp at Cor-pus Chris-ti to the place where San-ta An-na laid down his sword.

Grant went up a step or two in rank for his brave deeds at Mo-li-no del Rey and Cha-pul-te-pec, but his fame did not reach far.

He took a wife in the year 1848, and in 1854 made up his mind that he would war no more. He went to live on a farm of his own near St. Lou-is. Here he built his own house of hewn logs, did his own work, and led a life of peace. He was a poor man and could not hire help to do the work, and no doubt had a hard time, for it was a great change to lay down the gun and the sword, and turn from the field of strife, to take up the plough and the hoe and go to work in a hay-field or corn-patch.

So in 1860 Grant left his farm, and went to live at Ga-le-na, in the State of Il-li-nois. He was clerk in a store where hides were sold, and it is said that he was a good sales-man. Here he was when the war broke out in the U-ni-ted States, and the South and North, which had been as one, were two, and full of fierce hate.

For a long time in the South there had been a spark of hate, which did not burst out in a blaze till the 13th of A-pril, 1861, when an attack was made on Fort Sum-ter. The news spread like wild-fire. Men were quick to take sides. Some fought to save the dear old flag, and some fought to pull it down, and rend it in two.

BOM-BARD-MENT OF FORT SUM-TER.

Jeff-er-son Da-vis led the South. A-bra-ham Lin-coln, our chief, stood by the flag of the free—true, firm, brave, and good—and to him the whole North looked with faith that he would do the best he could for their cause.

CHAPTER III.

ON THE WAR-PATH.

LIN-COLN'S call for troops was made on the 15th of A-pril, 1861. On the 19th Grant went to work to drill a few of his towns-men in the use of the gun, and in a few days set off with them to Spring-field.

From there he wrote to one of the chief men at Wash-ing-ton that he would like to be made use of. He did not care where he was sent, or what rank he took, so long as he could use his skill and help to save the land from the foes that sought to take its life.

No word came back to him, so he staid at Spring-field to drill the troops that came in from all parts of the State. At the end of five weeks Cap-tain Grant was made Col-o-nel Grant and sent off to the seat of war at the head of a band of troops known as the Twen-ty First Ill-i-nois.

The Mis-sis-sip-pi Riv-er is full of queer turns and crooks, and at points here and there the men of the South made haste to set up forts and to fix troops to keep the North at bay. Ma-jor Gen-er-al Fre-mont had charge of all the troops in the far West, and in Sep-tem-ber, 1861, he sent Grant to Cai-ro, at the mouth of the O-hi-o, which was a strong point to guard. As soon as Grant reached Cai-ro he heard that Gen-er-al Polk, who had seized Co-lum-bus and Hick-man, on the Mis-sis-sip-pi, was on the way to Pa-du-cah, which he meant to take.

Fre-mont was at St. Lou-is. Grant sent word to him that he would start for Pa-du cah at haf-past six. He had to wait, for if Fre-mont said Grant must not go, he would have to stay where he was. No word came back on the wires, and so at half-past ten at night, on the 5th of Sep-tem-ber, he set out with two reg-i-ments and two gun-boats, and was at Pa-du-cah by half-past eight the next morn.

The men of the South, who were in gray, ran off, while the men in blue, led by Grant, made their way to the shore. Not a gun was fired. Grant took Pa-du-cah and all the flags and stores that were found in the place, and by this move kept the O-hi-o safe from the clutch of the foe.

At noon Grant went back to Cai-ro, and found there the word from Fre-mont for which he had not thought it best to wait. Fre-mont said he might take Pa-du-cah "if he had the strength"—that meant if he thought he had the men he would need for the fight there was no doubt would take place. Grant went at just the right time, and though some took him to task and thought he had not gone to work in the right way, the gain was so great that all else was soon lost sight of

For the next two months Grant kept a close watch on the three great streams that join in one and find their way at last to the Gulf of Mex-i-co. The men in gray were in great force at Co-lum-bus, and Grant had to move his troops from Pa-du-cah so as to get in the rear of the foe. He knew he could take Co-lum-bus, and it was hard for a man so quick to act to wait for the word to move.

Grant had charge of a lot of raw troops, men who had been brought up on farms, or had learned trades. None of them were skilled in the art of war, and though they might know how to shoot off a gun, and had been in bear hunts, and now and then on the red man's track, they were as green as they could be, but full of fight. On the 7th of No-vem-ber Grant moved his men and boats down to Hun-ter's Point, just out of range of the Co-lum-bus guns, and led his troops near Bel-mont, which was three miles off At this place the foe were

in camp, shut in by great trees that had been cut down to form a wall round the white tents.

Grant drew up his troops in line, and then sent out the whole force, in small bands, to fight the foe. Bel mont was cut up with sloughs and swamps, and here and there were dense woods, which made it hard work for those who did not know the ground. For four hours the fight was kept up, and all this time Grant was in the midst of the fire. It made the troops brave to see such brave men at their head. They drove the foe, foot to foot, through sloughs and fields, from tree to tree, down to the bank of the broad stream, back through the breast-works, seized a large force of men, and all the guns, and broke up the camp

Grant's troops were so wild with joy that they did all sorts of queer things, and were like such a lot of school boys that Grant, who saw that boats had set out from Co-lum-bus with a large force of men on board, gave the word to set the camps on fire. This drew on them a fire of guns from Co-lum-bus, which brought the men back to the ranks in great haste, and they took up their line of march to the boats.

In the mean-time the men in gray, whom the men in blue had not thought it worth while to watch, had crept down to the shore and were hid from sight by the high banks. Here, and in the woods close at hand, they met in small groups and made new plans. Fresh troops were sent to their aid from Co-lum-bus, and they took up their line of march in such a way that they were soon in front, in rear, and on all sides of Grant's men. It was a sad plight. Brave though they were, they did not see how they could get out of this trap in which they had been caught, and they thought there was but one thing to do, and that was to lay down their arms. But that was not Grant's way. One of his staff, to whom war was a new thing, rode up and with a pale face told of the fix they were in. "*Well,*" said Grant, "*if that is so, we must cut our way out as we cut our way in.*"

As soon as the troops found out that Grant meant to fight, they went to work with a will and soon drove the foe from the field, and then fled in great haste to their gun-boats. They thought this was the right thing to do, but it was not. And where do you think they left Grant? Why just near the corn-field where the Rebs were drawn up in line to fire on the gun-boats. He rode up on a knoll, and made a fine mark for the foe, who would have shot him down at once had they known who he was. As the day was cool Grant had put on the coat of one of his men, which hid his rank, and as he sat there on his horse he saw that it was no use to try to save his men who were out in search of those who had met with wounds in the fight, and that he would have a hard time to make his own way back to the gun-boats—which he might not reach.

THE ES-CAPE OF GRANT TO THE BOAT.

He set out at a slow pace so that the Rebs would not turn their fire on him, but as he drew near where his troops were he put spurs to his horse which slid down the bank, and was just in time to see his boats push off from the shore. He rode up as fast as he could, a plank was put out for him, and he went on board through a storm of shot.

Then the fire was kept up from the gun-boats till the last one was out of range, and there was no gain to the North or South.

Grant lost 485 men. Polk 642.

It was the first fight in which Grant took the lead.

A flag of truce is a white flag: a sign that the fight is at an end, and that peace reigns for a while.

The next day, Grant went out with a flag of truce and met one of his old West Point friends, who was on Gen-er-al Polk's staff. Grant told him how he rode out and met the foe.

"Was that you?" he said. "We saw you, and Gen-er-al Polk called to some of his troops: "Here, men, is a Yank, if you want to try your aim;" but all the men had their eyes on the boats and not one of them fired at Grant. But for that his first fight might have been his last one, and we should have heard no more of him.

CHAPTER IV.

FORT HEN-RY AND FORT DON-EL-SON.

Large fleets of gun-boats were in use in the West, in the first years of the war, and were sent up and down the streams with troops and stores. The Rebs were in great dread of them, and did their best to keep out of the range of their big guns. They were built so that not a man could be seen on them, and the shot and shell that were sent at them struck and did no harm

For two months Grant had been kept in one place but in Jan-u-a-ry, 1862, word was sent him that he might move his troops to the South, where it was thought there might be a fight. But no fight took place. The troops were out for more than a week, and were in great pain from the cold; and the storms of rain and snow that set in made some of them quite ill.

There are two great streams that branch out from the O-hi-o: the Ten-nes-see, which runs south, and the Cum-ber-land, which runs both south and east. At a bend in each of these streams the men of the South had built a strong-hold to keep back the men from the

North. Fort Hen-ry on the Ten-nes-see, and Fort Don-el-son on the Cum-ber-land, were like two great gate-ways which Lin-coln's troops would find hard to pass through.

But one of the men whom Grant sent out to see how the land lay in West Ken-tuck-y took a good look at Fort Hen-ry and sent back this word: "Two guns would make short work of the fort."

Grant at once made this fact known to his chief—Ma-jor Gen-er-al Hal-leck—who did not think it worth while to make an at-tack at that point. But Grant felt that the time had come to make a move, and he could not keep the thought off his mind. Six days was a long time for him to wait, so on the 28th of Jan-u-a-ry he sent word to St. Lou-is where Gen-er-al Hal-leck was: "By your leave I will take Fort Hen-ry on the Ten-nes-see, and fix and hold a large camp there." He was so sure of what he could do, that he did not say he would *try* to take the fort. The whole plan was clear to his own mind, and he was in haste to work it out.

On the 1st of Feb-ru-a-ry word came to Grant that he might move on the fort, and on the 2nd, he set out with a fleet of boats and a large force of men, and some of them went on shore on the east bank, eight miles from Fort Hen-ry. To make sure which was the best place to land, Grant went up in one of the gun-boats right in front of the fort, a shot from which was sent through the boat he was in. By this means he found out the range of the guns, and brought his troops up to a place three miles from the fort, and just out of reach of fire.

A strong and well-built fort was Fort Hen-ry, with twelve great guns on the front, and five more at the rear. A large force of men were in camp on the land side, and on the heights on the west bank was a small fort, known as Fort Hei-man.

It was late on the night of the 5th when Grant got his troops on shore, in a hard rain-storm. A flood had swept the land, and the fort was like an isle in the midst of a sea.

Grant's first plan was to seize Fort Hei-man and Fort Hen-ry at the same time, but the Rebs, when they saw what a force of men had been brought from Cai-ro made up their minds that they could not hold both works, so gave up Fort Hei-man and put all their strength in Fort Hen-ry.

Grant did not know this, for it was done at night; and on the next day he sent some of his troops out to seize the heights on the west bank. The rest were to move to the rear of Fort Hen-ry, "to charge and take the work by storm" as soon as he sent them word

Near the hour of noon the men took up their march. The gun-boats set out at the same time, and were soon in range of the fort. A sharp fire was kept up for an hour and a half, and at the end of that time the fort was in the hands of Grant's men.

Grant had thought to get round both forts and so hem the men in. But this could not be done. The men on foot had eight miles to march. They had to cut roads through the woods. Now and then they had to stop and build a bridge so that they could cross the streams the rains had made too deep to ford. Thus they lost an hour or two, and the troops in charge of the fort had a chance to run off to Fort Don-el-son.

Tilgh-man (*till-man*), who led the men from the South, staid with his guns to the last, and made a brave fight. The loss on both sides was small.

Grant at once sent word to Hal-leck, "*Fort Hen-ry is ours. I shall take Fort Don-el-son on the 8th.*" This he could not do, as the rains and the floods were so great; but by the 12th he had his troops in line of march, and by mid-day they were drawn up in front of the foe.

III.—THE AT-TACK ON FORT DON-EL-SON.

Fort Hen-ry was just twelve miles from Fort Don-el-son, which was on the west bank of the Cum-ber-land, north of the town of Do-ver. It was a strong fort at the top of a range of hills, out of reach it would seem of the foe, should they come by land or by boat. There were dense woods at the back of it, a deep gorge at one side, and all round the main fort were great breast-works to make it still more safe and strong.

Grant set to work to hem in Fort Don-el-son and all the troops it held, just as he had done at Fort Hen-ry. No troops came forth to stop his march, and on the night of the 13th he had brought his men and some of the wheel-guns up the heights on a line with the out-works of the foe, and from these points sent out shot now and then that they might know how near he was.

At sun-set of this day no fresh troops had come to his aid, and there were no gun-boats in sight. The night set in so cold that there was a fear the troops would all freeze to death. They did not dare to build fires. They had no tents—not much to eat—not a thing to wrap round them, and had to be on guard all night with their arms in their hands, for they were in point-blank range of the guns of the foe. A storm of snow and hail set in, and all night long could be heard the groans of the men who had been shot by the guns of those who stood at the out-posts of the fort to pick off those who came too near. Not a few of the men on both sides froze to death, if they did not die of their wounds.

By day-light on Fri-day, the 14th, the gun-boats in charge of Com-mo-dore Foote, came up the Cum-ber-land, and the troops from Fort Hen-ry, led by Brig-a-dier Gen-er-al Lew-is Wal-lace, were at once put in line.

This day Grant had word from his chief—Ma-jor Gen-er-al Hal-leck—to keep a large force at Fort Hen-ry, where he thought Grant and his men were. He did not know how much push there was in this man, who was in haste to bring the war to an end.

GUN-BOATS AT FORT DON-EL-SON.

At three o'clock on Fri-day the gun-boats made an at-tack on the fort, and brought down a storm of shot and shell that did them much harm. To add to this a gun burst on one of the boats. Com-mo-dore Foote was hurt and sent for Grant to come and see him. The night was cold. A wild storm of snow and sleet set in. The troops were not used to war, and it was hard for them to bear these ills.

By this time the men in the fort had made up their minds it was time for them to break through the line that Grant had drawn round them, and at dawn of Sat-ur-day—the 15th—while Grant was on board the flag-ship, they came out of their works and made an at-tack on the right of the line which was held by McAr-thur and McCler-nand. The men fought hard for hours, but there were more boys in gray than boys in blue, and McAr-thur had to give way at last. His loss was great. McCler-nand made out to hold his place till Lew. Wal-lace came up, and made the foe pay dear for what they had gained.

As Grant left the flag-ship at nine o'clock, he met an aide who rode up with great speed to tell him of the fight.

This was the first Grant knew of it. He put spurs to his horse, rode at once to the left where the fresh troops were—those who had not been in the fight—and told them to charge on the works. He and his staff told the men that the foe had tried to cut their way out and did not mean to stand a long siege. This gave the troops fresh strength, and they went straight to the front and "fought like brave men, one and all."

Two of the gun-boats ran up the stream and threw a few shells at long range, and all day long a hot fire was kept up. The boys in blue at last force their way through the lines and up the steep hill, while the guns from the fort keep up the fire that thins their ranks. They leap the ditch—but night comes on too soon for them to tell which side has won.

Some of those in the fort were wild to get out. They did not want to be caught like rats in a trap, and a large force led by men who stood high in rank crept out of the fort in the dark night and made their way to Nash-ville.

Gen-er-al Buck-ner was left in charge of Fort Don-el-son, and was too brave a man to shrink from the fate that was left for him and his troops. He sent one of his men with a note to Grant to ask his terms.

Grant said that he must sur-ren-der at once; and with a dash of his pen let him know what he meant to do:

ES-CAPE OF PRIS-ON-ERS AT FORT DON-EL-SON.

"*I pro-pose to move im-me-di-ate-ly on your works.*" Buck-ner did not like this, and sent word to Grant that the terms were too harsh. Grant went at once to see him. They had been good friends at West Point, and were good friends now, though one fought for the North and one for the South. Does it not seem strange? Grant told Buck-ner that he had no wish to take down his pride in a mean way, so he and his staff might keep their swords, and they and all of the men might take off such goods as they had had for their own use. But they must give up all that the U-ni-ted States had a right to.

The cap-ture of Fort Don-el-son was the first great deed that had been done since the war broke out. It gave good cheer to the North, and put U-lys-ses S. Grant in the front rank of fame.

CHAPTER V.

TWO DAYS OF BLOOD.

THE North had now two strong-holds—one on the Ten-nes-see—and one on the Cum-ber-land. Day by day fresh troops were sent from the East, and in Feb-ru-a-ry a large force of men, in charge of Grant, set out to push their way to West Ten-nes-see. It was a slow march, for the Ten-nes-see rose so high that there were but two or three bluffs where the boats could land. Troops were left at each of these points, while Grant—who at this time was thought to be far too bold—kept on, and made a halt at Shi-loh, on the east bank of the stream. From this point he could keep an eye on the rail-road that ran through the heart of the South, and vex the foe, which was then in great force at or near Co-rinth.

By the first of A-pril both sides were full of fight, and each grew more and more bold.

Shi-loh was just a log-church that stood on a ridge of ground from two and a half to three miles back from the bluffs at Pitts-burgh Land-ing, with Snake creek

SHI-LOH CHURCH.

on the north, and Lick creek on the south, and Owl creek on the west. All these creeks, which for the most part of the year were of no great size, were now broad streams. Here and there were thick woods, a high bluff, or a deep gorge, and the men had to make the most of these as they were new to war, and had had no chance to learn how to dig the trench, to throw up earth-works, or to build such forts as might serve them in a time of need.

Grant, who had to keep an eye on all the troops, and to see to their needs, spent each day at Pitts-burgh Land-ing, and at night went down in the boat to Sa-van-na. Sher-man was in charge of the troops at the front, with their lines drawn up to face the Co-rinth road, by which route the Rebs would have to come.

Shots were fired now and then from both sides, and by the 3rd of A-pril the fight seemed close at hand.

Grant staid on the field till quite late each night, up to the time the fight took place. On Fri-day, the 4th, while on his way to the front, his horse fell with him. The night was dark, the rain poured down, and he had to trust to his horse to find the road. Grant's leg was hurt so that his boot had to be cut off, and for two or three days he was quite lame.

No one knew just at what point the foe would make the first at-tack, but Grant, up to this time, had thought it might be at Crump's Land-ing. By the 5th he was quite sure that the fight would take place at Shi-loh, and at once went to work to place his troops so that they could come from the right or left flank to the aid of those who were at the front.

Some of those who led the troops had not been in this kind of a fight, and did not know the rules of war, so they went to the left when they should have gone to right, and were not where they should have been when the fight took place.

At dawn, on the 6th of A-pril, Gen-er-al Al-bert Sid-ney Johns-ton, who led the troops from the South, made a fierce at-tack on the lines at Shi-loh. Grant

THE REB-EL GEN AL-BERT SID-NEY JOHN-STON KILL-ED.

had gone to Sa-van-na, six miles off, and as soon as he heard the fire of the guns he made his way at once to the front. The fight was hot from the first, and as the Rebs came up they fell on the guards sent out by Pren-tiss and Sher-man who soon had their troops in line.

These two chiefs had a lot of raw men from the West who knew how to use a pick, axe, or spade, but did not know well how to load or fire a gun. Part of them fled in great fright to the rear. The rest stood firm. New lines had to be made as the ranks gave way.

If all those who led the troops had been as brave as Grant and Sher-man, the souls of the men would have been fired with strength, and they would not have fought so like an armed mob. But, as I have said, war was a new thing, and all these men had much to learn.

It was not strange that they were full of fear, that their hearts gave way, and that they lost their heads.

All day the fight went on, with great loss on both sides. Now and then the boys in blue had had to fall back and to change their lines, and when night came on they were more than a mile from the place where they had stood at dawn of the day to meet the foe.

In one of the moves Gen-er-al Pren-tiss did not fall back with the rest, and he and a large force of his men fell in the hands of the Rebs.

Sher-man was shot twice; once in the hand, once near the neck. A third ball went through his hat. More than one horse was shot from un-der him. It would have been a sad day for the troops at Shi-loh had Sher-man had to leave the field.

A hard rain set in on the night of the 6th. The Yanks had lost all their tents—the Rebs were in their camp—and they had to rest as best they could. Grant's leg gave him so much pain that he could not rest, so he went to the log-church. Here men were brought in to have their wounds dressed, or to have an arm or a leg cut off. This was a sight he could not bear, so he limped back to the tree 'neath which he sat to wait for the dawn of day.

IV.—BAT-TLE OF SHI-LOH.

Four times each hour all through the night the gun-boats sent a shell right down near the foe; and all night long the boats brought fresh troops, with brave men at their head, to the east side of the stream to swell the ranks of the boys in blue.

GRANT A-SLEEP.

Grant had made up his mind to whip the Rebs the next day, and he had found out that the side which made the first at-tack was the side that won the fight.

This was the way he ranged his men:—

Gen-er-al Lew. Wal-lace on the right, Sher-man to his left; then McCler-nand, and then Hurl-but. Nel-son of Bu-ell's corps (*kor*) was on the left; Crit-ten-den next in line, and on his right; and McCook at the far end of the right wing.

Nel-son led the fight on the 7th, and soon the whole line was in the heat of the fray. The strength of the new troops told at once. The Rebs were not so full of dash as they had been on the first day. They were worn out. So were Grant's men; but they were full of pluck, and pluck is bound to win.

Ground was won and lost on both sides. The dead lay in heaps; blue and gray side by side. But the Rebs were pushed inch by inch till they had lost all they had gained. As the day wore on it was plain to be seen that the fight was near its end; the Rebs would have to yield. A large force of their men had gone to the rear.

THE LAST CHARGE AT SHI-LOH

At three o'clock *Charge!* was the cry that went out to the boys in blue. They met it with loud cheers, held their guns in front of them, and with a run drove the foe quite off the field.

On the 6th there were 33.000 boys in blue at Shi-loh. On the 7th Bu-ell brought 20.000 more. It is said that Beau-re-gard, who led the foe, had 40,955. Our loss in the two days' fight was 12.217. Theirs, 10.699.

On the 8th, when Beau-re-gard sent to Grant to know if he could take his dead from the field and place them in the ground, he found that Grant had done this kind act. Foes had the same care as friends. Had Grant been a hard, bad man, he would not have done such a deed as this, which is not a part of the code of war, and it was proof that he had a large heart, full of peace and good-will to all men.

CHAPTER VI.

THE SIEGE OF CO-RINTH.

Up to this time Grant had thought, as most of the North did, that the war would soon be at an end; that men would lay down their guns and swords, and go back to the work they had left and the peace they had known.

But the cause for which the South fought was one they had thought of for a long time. For years and years they had kept up a talk of State rights, and their own wrongs, and at last they had got to feel that the North was their worst foe. There were bad men on both sides who did all they could to fan this flame which took fire in 1861.

The South had made the war—and the North must do its best to crush it out. So Grant thought, and was in haste to bring back peace to the land. The next we hear of him is at Co-rinth, to which place he laid siege on the last of May. It was thought there would be a great fight at this place, but there was none at all. The Rebs went out, and when the boys in blue went in they found a lot of old guns made of wood, and all round signs that Beau-re-gard had not such a strong force as he was thought to have had.

For the next two or three months there was not much done by the troops in West Ten-nes-see. The war went on in the East, and much blood was shed.

On the 15th of Sep-tem-ber Price came up from the South and seized I-u-ka, which is a score of miles east of Co-rinth. On the 15th Grant sent word to Hal-leek that by his leave he would at-tack Price ere he could cross Bear Creek. On the 18th he sent Gen-er-al Ord up to a point four miles from I-u-ka, where he found a strong force of the Rebs on the north side of the town.

Rose-crans was to push up on the left with all speed so that the at-tack could take place on the 19th. The next day they might have to fall back as there was a fear that Van Dorn, who had come up to the aid of Price, would at-tack Co-rinth. His plan was to cross the Ten-nes-see and make his way to Ken-tuck-y. This Grant did not mean to let him do.

The roads were so bad that Rose-crans could not get his troops near I-u-ka as soon as he had planned, and Ord had to wait till he came. The Rebs were on a hill which gave them a view of the road, and as Rose-crans came up with his men at half-past four they at once made a fierce at-tack on the boys in blue and drove them back. There was no chance for them to use their field-guns—two or three of which they lost—or to fight as they would if they had had more space, but they held their own till dark, and had strong hopes that I-u-ka would fall in their hands the next day.

The wind did not blow the right way to bear the sound of the guns to Ord, who was some miles off, and so he did not know of the fight at the time it took place. Late at night he got the word, and at once set out with his troops to help Rose-crans and Ham-il-ton. But the Rebs had found out that they would soon be hemmed in by Grant's troops, and so took flight by a back road while the way was still free. At nine o'clock the next day, when Grant got back to I-u-ka, for he had to drive up the troops on all sides, he found the foe had fled, and were by this time so far off that there was no chance to catch them.

This small fight at I-u-ka put a check on the plans of the South, and drove the Rebs back to Co-rinth—where they made an at-tack on the 2nd of Oc-to-ber. On the 3rd the fight was hot and fierce, and Van Dorn won the day. This piece of good-luck made the boys

AT-TACK ON CO-RINTH.

in gray more bold. They stormed the earth works, and fought their way up to the town. A sharp fire from the forts drove them back and put them to rout. Twice—thrice—they charge in the same way, and are met with a storm as brave as their own. At last they give up, by noon the fight is at an end, the foe is in flight, and the Stars and Stripes wave once more from the fort in Co-rinth.

It was Grant's plan to push on at once, seize Van Dorn's force and end the war in that part of the land.

But the troops were worn out with the two days' fight. Rose-crans plead their need of rest, and his own, and was glad to sheathe his sword for a while. He had won a great fight, and he had his meed of fame. He was made a Ma-jor Gen-er-al, and put in com-mand of the ar-my of the Cum-ber-land.

Grant was such a plain man that it was hard work for him to get those who put on more style to do as he bade them, or to yield him the praise that was his due. They had no great faith in his skill, and thought that all he had done and won had been through sheer good luck. But he was calm through all, and could bide his time. He did not love war. The great cry of his heart was "Let us have peace!" His whole thought was how to bring this strife to an end.

The Mis-sis-sip-pi is a great stream that starts in the North West and makes its way down to the Gulf of Mex-i-co. It was the great prize for which the North and South fought, and the South who knew it would be death to their cause to lose it, had, when the war first broke out, built forts on the best points the whole length of the stream. Co-lum-bus, Fort Pil-low, and Isl-and (*i-land*) Num-ber Ten, they lost in the spring of 1862. Vicks-burg and Port Hud-son were still in their hands, and it was Grant's wish to move on Vicks-burg and take it as he took Fort Don-el-son.

The North had seized New-Or-leans, and in June 1862, Com-mo-dore Far-ra-gut and Brig-a-dier Gen-er-al Thom-as Wil-li-ams made their way up the Mis-sis-sip-pi as far as Vicks-burg, but did not take the town.

The South then set to work to add to the strength of the fort on both sides, and made it so strong that it was thought no force could take it by land or by sea. Those who tried were sure to fail, and as long as Vicks-burg stood, the South could keep the North at bay. The whole of the Mis-sis-sip-pi was theirs.

CHAPTER VII.

THE SIEGE OF VICKS-BURG.

THE town of Vicks-burg stands on a high cliff on the east bank of the Mis-sis-sip-pi, and high bluffs edge the stream for at least a score of miles. So steep were these cliffs that no guns could be brought to bear on them, and no boats from the North could pass the forts and make their way out to the sea.

In the rear of Vicks-burg the ground was rough and steep. Here and there was a deep, dark gorge. The low lands were full of creeks and swamps. All these were a great help to the South who flung out its flag, and dared the whole North to haul it down and set up the Stars and Stripes in its place.

Grant kept his eye on Vicks-burgh. He knew it would be a hard task to get near it, or to take it, but he did not mind that. He set his brain to work to think out a plan by which he could get round the foe. Both he and his troops were sick of camp-life. It would soon be time for them to be on the move.

Grant thought if he could get back of the Rebs, on the

crest of the hills, he would force them to fight in the field or leave them to starve. But the long rains and the bad roads made him give up this plan. Then he thought a ditch could be cut which would change the course of the Mis-sis-sip-pi and let the gun-boats pass by Vicks-burg in full view of the forts, but out of reach of their guns.

CA-NAL AT VICKS-BURG.

In Jan-u-a-ry he set his troops to work out this scheme—which Lin-coln thought a good one. The eyes of the North and South were on him. For two months the work was kept up, and it was thought a new route might at last be made. But in March the Mis-sis-sip-pi rose to a great height. The strong dams that had been built could not stay its course. All the camps and all the live stock were swept off by the flood, and the troops had to flee for their lives. The work of all those weeks was lost, and

Grant made up his mind that Vicks-burg must be won by hard fights. All these new schemes and new routes would help him get a foot-hold, and give work to his men till such time as he could move his troops on dry land.

While this sort of work went on, Ad-mi-ral Far-ra-gut, with a part of his fleet, ran by the forts at Port Hud-son, and came up near where Grant was. For a while he lay near War-ren-ton, but could not give much aid to Grant, who was at a loss to know what to do.

The North thought him slow, and had a mind to send a new man to take his place. But Lin-coln had faith in him, and said, "Wait. Give him a chance."

It was on the night of the 16th of A-pril, 1863, that Grant set out with Ad-mi-ral Por-ter to take the town of Vicks-burg. The night was dark; there was no moon; and by ten o'clock the fleet were all in line, and one by one slipped down the stream as far as Mil-li-ken's bend. Soon a fire of shot and shell came down on them from the bluffs. The boats sent back their fire, and kept close to the shore where the smoke would hide them best. Fires were lit on the bluffs that made all up and down the stream as light as day. The tides were swift, and the glare of lights, and the dense smoke made it hard for the men at the helm to steer the boats. The Hen-ry Clay, which had in tow a barge with troops on board, had to be cut loose and was soon set on fire by a shell that burst near it.

For more than two hours the fleet were in the fight: but at last the blaze on hill and stream died out, the noise of the guns ceased, and all was still and dark once more.

On the 26th of A-pril six more boats with troops on board, tried to run by the Vicks-burg forts. Five of them got by, but one was struck in the hull by a large ball and sunk at once. By the 29th the whole of the Thir-teenth corps (*kor*) was at a place known as Hard-Times. The plan was to get on Pem-ber-ton's left—and at-tack the fort at Grand Gulf.

On the 29th, Ad-mi-ral Por-ter brought his gun-boats in front of Grand Gulf, but though they kept up their fire for more than five hours, they had to turn back at last. The guns of the foe were too much for them. But that night the boats ran by the forts at Grand Gulf and all the troops that were on board were put on shore at Hard Times, and were soon on their march to De Shroon's, a point on the west-shore, three miles down the stream.

Grant found out there was a good road from Bru-ins-

GUN-BOATS ON THE MIS-SIS-SIP-PI.

burg to Port Gib-son, so he at once made up his mind to cross the Mis-sis-sip-pi and move on Grand Gulf from the rear. On the 1st of May they met the foe near Port Gib-son and drove them from the field. Now and then they had to stop to build a bridge, or to have a brush with the foe, and in this way they kept on their march to Grand Gulf They went in camp with Pem-ber-ton at Vicks-burg on the left-flank, and Jo-seph E. Johns-ton at Jack-son on their right-flank. Grant's first move was to Jack-son, and on the 14th of May Sher-man and McPher-son's corps took it by storm, and left not a thing there that could be of use to the foe.

The next day the troops went west-ward, and on the 16th met the foe at Cham-pi-on's hill where a hard fight was fought.

V.--BAT-TLE OF CHAM-PION HILLS.

The boys in blue drove back the boys in gray, and on the 17th, came up with them at the Big Black. Here they fought hard for two or three hours. The North took the works by storm, and the foe fled in great haste, and the next day Grant had his troops in front of Vicks-burg.

CAP-TURE OF A GUN.

For three weeks the men had not had much to eat, and now they felt the need of bread. As Grant went through the ranks one day, one of the men who knew him said in a low voice, but so that Grant could hear him—"*Hard-tack.*" The men took it up and "*Hard-tack! hard-tack!* hard-tack!" was the cry the whole length of the line. As soon as Grant told them that a new road had been built by which food would be brought to them, the cry for bread gave way to cheers, and all went well.

Grant sent word that the at-tack should be made on Vicks-burg by all parts of the line at the same hour on the 22nd of May. So at 10 a.m. they made the charge, and a fierce one it was. Some of the brave men made their way up to the works, and set their flags there, but found no place where they could get in. It was hard work to drag the field-guns up and down the steep

FIRST CHARGE AT VICKS-BURG.

slopes in the face of such a rain of shot and shell as was sent from the breast-works that hid the foe, so they could be of no use in this close fight.

Grant's loss was great, and on the night of the 22nd the troops were with-drawn, and for two days the dead were left on the field in the hot sun, as it was not safe for live men to go near them. The stench was so great that Pem-ber-ton knew that all the folks in Vicks-burg would soon be made sick by it, and he had his troops cease their fire so that Grant's men could dig graves and care for the slain.

Grant did not want to lose more men than there was need to lose, and he saw there was not much to be made in this kind of a fight. There was but one thing to do, and that was to out-camp the foe.

This is known as the siege of Vicks-burg, and I will tell you how the boys in blue went to work to starve out the boys in gray. Here a trench must be dug. There a wall must be put up. On top of these walls were great sand-bags, with a space left as a loop-hole for a gun. Logs were put on top of the bags so that the men could stand up and not be seen by the foe, and hit by their guns. For all this time the fire was kept up with shot and shell, and a sharp watch was kept up on both sides.

All the roads that led to and from Vicks-burg were held by the troops from the North. They seized the live stock, and all the corn they could find on the roads, and fresh troops came from Mis-sou-ri and elsewhere to add to their strength. There was no chance for Pem-ber-ton to send word to Johns-ton, or for Johns-ton to send word to Pem-ber-ton.

Mines were cut deep in the hills, some of which were blown up and left chasms where they had stood. The Rebs would dig on their side, but did not strike the line just right so as to push in where the boys in blue were at work.

"Once," says Grant, "when a charge went off there were a few men at work in the mine that had been cut through to find ours. All that were there were thrown in the air, and some of them came down on our side—more scared than hurt. One of these was a black man. Some one asked him how high he went up. 'Dun no,' he said, 'but t'ink bout t'ree mile.' Gen-er-al Lo-gan took charge of this black man, and made good use of him till the end of the siege."

THROW-ING HAND GRE-NADES.

The Mis-sis-sip-pi,

VI.–THE SIEGE OF VICKS-BURG. THE CRA-TER.

from its source to its mouth—save the point right in front of Vicks-burg and of Port Hud-son—was in the hands of the North. The land far and near had been laid waste to feed the large force of troops out-side of Vicks-burg.

Pem-ber-ton had said "I knew I could stand a siege," and it was his wish to hold the fort as long as there was a man left to fire a gun. But there were those in Vicks-burg who felt that it was best to run up the white flag. To hold out meant to starve, and the need of food was so great that death seemed to stare them in the face.

Deep caves were dug in which they had to make their homes so as to be safe from the shells that were sent in-to the town. In time these were not fit to live in. The place was full of tramps—men who would eat all they could get, but would not work. Worse ills than these they had to put up with, and hope had ceased to cheer them. Day by day there was less and less food. An egg was worth its weight in gold. Mule meat could be bought, but it was dear, and some could not eat it at all.

One day as Grant rode round his lines he stopped for a drink at a house where a proud dame dwelt, whose heart was all with the South. She asked him with a sneer if he thought he should get in to Vicks-burg. "Yes, of course," said Grant. "But when?" asked the dame. "I can not tell just when I shall take the town," said Grant in his calm way, but *I mean to stay here till I do if it takes me thir-ty years.*"

At this the proud dame's heart went down, down, down. She had been full of hope that her side would win, but if this man meant to keep up the siege for such a length of time—and she knew by his looks that he meant what he said—what chance was there? Its fate was sure, as time would show.

On the 1st of July, Johns-ton made a move in hopes to turn Grant's troops, and give Pem ber-ton a chance to cut his way out. He fixed his camp 'twixt Browns-ville and the Big Black, and wrote a note to Pem-ber-ton that the move he had made was the best one, he thought, to raise the siege of Vicks-burg.

But the note, and Johns-ton too, fell in the hands of Grant's men, and on the 3rd of Ju-ly white flags were put up on part of the works round Vicks-burg. The fight on that part of the line came to an end at once. Soon two men were seen on their way to the camp with white flags.

The news spread! The troops were wild with joy! All they had borne had not been in vain! The siege was at an end, and once more the Stars and Stripes would wave from the heights of Vicks-burg!

The two men were Bow-en and Mont-gom-e-ry, Pem-ber-ton's aide-de-camps. It was their wish to speak to

Grant. But Grant would not see them. He sent word that if it was Pem-ber-ton's wish he would meet him in front of McPherson's corps at three o'clock that same day.

So at three o'clock Pem-ber-ton came with Bow-en and Mont-gom-er-y, and Grant with Gen-er-als Ord, McPher-son, Lo-gan, A. J. Smith, and some of his staff. They met near an old oak-tree, and at the end of an hour's talk had not come to terms.

By ten o'clock that night Grant was to send his terms to the foe, who would then say what they would do. Grant wrote out his terms, and said at the close that if they were such as to please the foe, "white flags must be put up on all your lines so that my troops shall not fire on your men"

MEET-ING OF GRANT AND PEM-BER-TON

The Sur-ren-der of Vicks-burg took place on the 4th of Ju-ly. It was a grand but yet a sad sight. Not a cheer was heard as men in gray filed out and stocked their arms in front of the men in blue.

A man in blue went through the town at a slow pace. He led the van-guard of Grant's troops. This is the way they took the town. First came one man. Then there was a space. Then three men. Then a space. Then six men. These were a part of the van-guard. Then came all the rest of the troops—a mass of blue coats.

Lo-gan s corps was the first to march in to the town. The For-ty Fifth Il- li-nois was at the head, and put its torn flag on the court house of Vicks-burg.

Grant, with his staff, rode in to town at the head of Lo-gan's corps. He was proud of his troops—proud of what he had done—not for the fame it brought him, but as proof that he was right when all thought he was wrong. His praise rang through the land. Votes of thanks, and gifts of great cost were sent to him. He was made a Ma-jor Gen-er-al. Lin-coln wrote to thank him for what he had done.

The loss of Vicks-burg was a great blow to the South. Get-tys-burg fell the same day. Hope left their hearts, but they still fought on, as grim and stern as knights of old.

CHAPTER VIII.

AT CHAT-TA-NOO-GA.

THE State of Ten-nes-see is full of hills and vales. Great rail-roads run through it from the north and the south, and from the east to the west. But few slaves were in the state when the war broke out, and the white folks who dwelt there felt their hearts drawn to the North.

Where the rail-roads from Mem-phis and Charles-ton, Rich-mond, Nash-ville, and At-lan-ta met, a town sprang up which took its name from the mount at whose base it was built.

This was the town of Chat-ta-noo-ga.

Mis-sion-a-ry Ridge was at the south-east. Look-out Moun-tain at the west.

Grant's next move was to Chat-ta-noo-ga, for all the grain and beef from Geor-gi-a, Flor-i-da, and Al-a ba-ma, that was sent to feed the troops at the North, had to pass through this place, and if it fell in the hands of the foe the boys in blue would soon starve to death.

While Grant was in front of Vicks-burg, Rose-crans

had had a fight with Bragg at Chick-a-mau-ga in which he met with great loss, and if Thom-as had not come to his aid he could not have held Chat-ta-noo-ga.

On the 9th of Sep-tem-ber the boys in blue took the town, and drove Bragg back to the hill tops, Mis-sion-a-ary Ridge and Look-out Moun-tain, whence he sent shells in the camp at the foot of the hills.

All through the month of Sep-tem-ber, the Ar-my of the Cum-ber-land lay in Chat-ta-noo-ga, in a state of siege. The foe were on the hills all round them. There was no chance for them to cut their way out.

The days were hot, and the nights were cold. They had no change of clothes, no great coats, and no wraps to keep them warm when they slept. They had but few tents. Food was scarce. Then the fall rains set in. There was no grass, hay, or oats for mule or horse, and the poor beasts lay dead in all the camp streets. Men died of their wounds, who might have got well if they had had the right kind of care.

All that Bragg had to do was to wait, and Chat-ta-noo-ga would fall in his hands.

None of the boys in blue were in such straits as these through all the four years of the war.

It was late in Oc-to-ber, 1863, when Grant took his

place at the head of the Ar-my of the Cum-ber-land. He sent word to hold Chat-ta-noo-ga. Thom-as sent word back "*I will hold the town till I starve!*"

On the 20th he set out from Lou-is-ville by rail, was at Nash-ville the same night, and at Chat-ta-noo-ga the 22nd. His first care had been to send food to the troops, of which they were in great need.

Burn-side was in East Ten-nes-see. Hook-er at Bridge-port. Sher-man and his corps were on the way to join Grant, who at once went to work to lay out his plans. Troops were sent from each corps to guard the roads, and a force, in charge of Giles A. Smith, to seize a range of hills which would give them a strong post on high ground.

The night of the 26th was dark and thick with fog. At dawn of the next day three-score flat boats full of troops set out from Chat-ta-noo-ga. The tide was so strong there was no need of oars, and as they kept close to the lee shore they were not seen nor heard by the foe, till they came to the land on the south side of the stream.

Here a slight fight took place, but by five o'clock Smith had his troops on the hills. Four or five of his men had wounds, but no one was killed.

On the 26th Hook-er's corps crossed the Ten-nes-see at Bridge-port, and took up their line of march, by way of White-sides to Wau-hatch-ie. The guards in front of the foe fell back as Hook-er and his troops went on. Bragg's men on the hills sent shells down on the men in the vale. But Hooker kept on, and on the 28th went in camp with-in a mile of the place where Smith was, though on low ground. That night Long-street's corps made a fierce at-tack on Gea-ry at Wau-hatch-ie. How-ard came up to aid Gea-ry, who for three hours had kept up the fight by the light of the moon, and the flash of fire-arms. By four o'clock the fight was at an end and the foe sent back at each point.

How-ard, while on his way, came on a range of hills which lay in his line of march. They were steep, and all up the sides was a dense growth of trees. On top the foe had built strong earth works, as if they meant to stay there for some time. How-ard and his men scale the walls. Shot and shell pour down on them from the guns of the foe. They do not mind. Up, up, up they climb, take the works by storm, seize a large force of men, and help to turn the tide of war.

For the next week or two Grant had his hands full. He had to clear all the roads, see that the troops were well fed, get all his troops in line and add strength to his force so that he could drive the foe from the hills round Chat-ta-noo-ga.

On the 14th of No-vem-ber, Grant sent word to Burn-side to hold Long-street in check, to give him (Grant) time to put a force 'twixt him and Bragg that would make Long-street take to the hill roads to get at the stores he would need.

The next day he sent word to Burn-side to hold Knox-ville for at least one week. On the 22d he heard that Bragg had left Mis-sion-a-ry Ridge, and the next day the guns in Fort Wood and all the small forts gave the sign that the troops were to march on the foe.

Gen-er-al Gor-don Gran-ger had charge of Fort Wood, with Gen-er-al Phil Sher-i-dan and his troops on the right, and Gen-er-al Wood and his men on the left. At a sign they all went to the plain in front and on the right of Fort Wood.

The sun broke through the fog that had lain all day in the vale and lit the guns of the troops so that they shone and flashed as if tipped with fire.

At first the foe on the hill-tops thought this was just a side-show, but when they saw the boys in blue move through the strip of woods that led up the hills, they knew what was meant.

Ere Bragg had had time to send troops from his main camp on the ridge Sher-i-dan had seized his grand guards and was in strong force in the new posts they had won. All day long the fight was kept up. The foe were swept back from the points they had held, and at night-fall the great hosts slept in peace on the heights.

Sher-man had tried hard to get up to Grant, but the roads were so bad, and the streams so hard to cross, that it was not till the night of the 23rd that his third corps came to the mouth of the South Chick-a-mau-ga, four miles north of Chat-ta-noo-ga. The Chick-a-mau-ga is quite broad at this point and the bridge train could not bring the boats up in time for the troops to cross with much speed.

Saw-mills were run night and day, and boats made and brought up through the woods out of sight of the foe. A lot of these bridge boats were hid in North Chick-a-mau-ga creek, five miles north of the mouth of the South Chick-a-mau-ga, and on the night of the 23rd of No-vem-ber a large force of armed men was brought down to a point near the mouth of the South Chick-a-mau-ga.

A small force went on shore, and with great speed made its way up the bank and seized a score of the out-guard, and in a short time the North had a strong hold on the south bank of the Ten-nes-see.

CHARGE AT MIS-SION-A-RY RIDGE.

A bridge of boats was built so that the troops could cross this stream, and take up their line of march as Grant thought best. Sher-man made his way to the foot-hills,

VII.—BAT-TLE A-MONG T K-

up which he went, and was soon on top, and not a man was hurt. At night the light from his camp-fires made it known to friend and foe that he had seized and held Mis-sion-a-ry Ridge.

Hook-er's camps were all on the west side of Look-out creek. On the Chat-ta-noo-ga side of Look-out mount, was a zig-zag road. Hook-er thought if he could gain this road he could drive off the foe so they could not get aid from Bragg.

The mount was steep and rough. Great crags stuck out on all sides. Few would care to climb this wall of stone, and who would dare such a task in face of the foe, and of the fire of those great guns? It makes us hold our breath to read of such brave deeds.

Up the face of the steep hill go Gea-ry and his troops. They drive back the foe; they pass the guns; they round the peak. Up go Hook-er and his brave men; and for hours the fire is kept up on both sides. There are two or three sharp fights, but at last they drive the foe from their walls and pits, and get a foot-hold on a piece of flat-land. At two o'clock in the day it was too dark to keep up the fight. The clouds hung low. A thick fog rose from the vale. The guns sent forth flame and smoke. Now and then, as the fog rose or fell, a flag could be seen. Now and then a flash through the clouds gave a hint of where the fight was and how it went oh.

At four o'clock Hook-er sent word to his chief that the prize was won. Look out Moun-tain was theirs! and the hills shook with the fire of joy the guns sent forth.

And where was Grant all this time? At Or chard knoll, which was on a low range of hills half way 'twixt Chat-ta-noo-ga and Mis-sion-a-ry Ridge. From this point he could see all that took place, and could send help to those who were in need of it. But though much had been done there was still much to do. The foe, with Bragg at their head, were still in force on Mis-sion-a-ry Ridge. Sher-man and his troops were on a spur of this ridge, but a deep gorge lay twixt him and the point of the hill where Bragg and his corps were.

Not a house, not a tree, nor so much as a fence was to be seen in the vale, which had been made in-to one great camp-ground. All the troops were on the hills, where earth-works, and breast-works of logs, had been thrown up to make each point as strong as a fort.

On the 24th of No-vem-ber, in the night, the foe leave Look-out Moun-tain, cross Chat-ta-noo-ga creek, burn each bridge, and set their camps on fire, and make their way to Mis-sion-a-ry Ridge to swell Bragg's force.

At dawn of the 25th Grant had all his troops in place, and soon the horn was blown that told them all to charge on the foe. Sher-man, was still on a hill near the main ridge, and on the right flank of Bragg's corps.

Cock-rell, Al-ex-an-der, and Light-burn were to hold this hill; Corse was to act on the right of the front; Mor-gan L. Smith was to move on the east base of the ridge; and Loo-mis on the west base. Up the face of the hill went this great force of troops; up to one end of the earth-works from which they drove the boys in gray, till they got firm foot-hold on the crest of the ridge.

Sher-man kept up such a close fire on the right flank that Bragg had to turn his front that way. This gave Grant the right kind of a chance. He was in hopes that just such a move would take place. Hook-er had made haste down from the top of Look-out but had had to stop at Chick-a-mau-ga creek to build the bridge the foe had burnt, and so did not come up in time to aid in the as-sault.

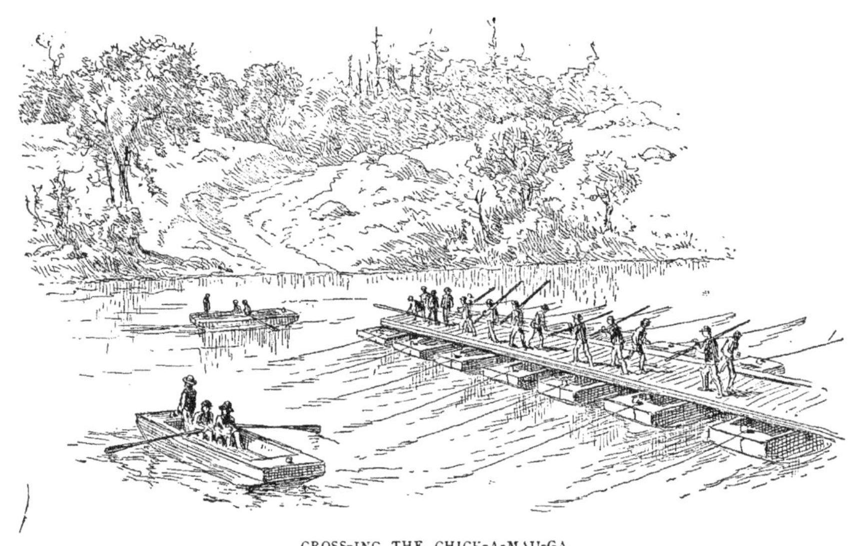

CROSS-ING THE CHICK-A-MAU-GA.

All up the ridge, from the base to the top, were lines of pits full of men and guns. The troops, as soon as the horn blew, made a dash at the first line of the foe and took it by storm; not a gun was fired. Up, up they climb. Wild shouts ring all through the line. Shot and shell rain on them from the fort at the top. They have to lie down and crawl on their hands and knees. Turn back? No! None of the men who fought with Grant had such a thought in their minds. They must take what they set out to win, or die on the way.

Here and there on the heights a flag is set. So much gain. When Sher-i-dan saw these flags go up he knew that the North would win.

Bragg and his men fought hard but when they saw these troops pour in-to the earth-works in such crowds saw them rise at the same time on the top of six hills they felt as if their cause was lost. Hosts of them threw down their arms. Hosts of them fled head-long down the slope. The troops threw stones at them, as they could not take the time to load their guns.

Bragg and his staff strove to get their men in line. But all in vain. A few came back, but they could not be put to much use, so in the night they all fled by one of the rear roads, and Chat-ta-noo-ga was safe. The troops went in-to camp that night with glad hearts, and their cheers were heard for miles and miles.

Thom-as lost	4,000, men.
Sher-man	1,500, men.
Hook-er	1,500, men.

CHAPTER IX.

THE BAT-TLE OF THE WIL-DER-NESS.

The North was loud in praise of U-lys-ses S. Grant. His name and fame were known through-out the land. He was made Lieu-ten-ant Gen-er-al, and had charge of 500.000 men in the field. Lin-coln wrote to him—"*You have brave men, and a just cause, and may God give you strength.*"

God did give him strength, for no one man could

have done what Grant did with-out the aid of Him who is an arm of aid to the weak.

I did not stop to tell you of the fight at Knox-ville, which Burn-side won. He drove Long-street out as far as Rus-sel-ville, and tried his best to get him and his men quite out of East Ten-nes-see. But they went in camp for the next three months, as no more fights could take place till the spring of the year.

On the 3rd of March, Grant was sent for to come to Wash-ing-ton; and on the 10th he went back to the front. He had been with the Ar-my of the Ten-nes-see, the Ar-my of the Mis-sis-sip-pi, the Ar-my of the Cum-ber-land, and now he was with new troops that made up the Ar-my of the Po-to-mac.

Sher-man did not like this change, and wrote to Grant: "Don't stay in Wash-ing-ton. Come West. Let us make it dead-sure. Here you are at home; you know your ground; you know us and we know you."

But Grant felt that he ought to go to Vir-gin-i-a, where the foe were now in great force with Rob-ert E. Lee at their head. He soon had his plans laid. "On to Rich-mond!" was the war-cry that rang through the North and the hearts of men were fired with fresh zeal. Fresh troops were sent to the front.

Through March and A-pril Grant was at Cul-pep-er, whence he could send word to all the troops on land and sea. They were made to close in on the North, the South, the East, and the West, so that in case of need they could be brought well up to the front by a quick march.

CROSS-ING THE RAP-I-DAN.

Lee was in a strong place on the south bank of the Rap-i-dan, with the Blue Ridge at his left. On the right was a wil-der-ness of trees where were a few roads, much like—foot-paths through a lot of brush-wood. At the rear were Long-street and his troops, some of them on horse-back.

Grant's first plan was to force or tempt the foe out of their works to fight, so he made a plunge in-to the Wil-der-ness on the 4th of May, 1864.

The Rebs were at once up and in arms, and on the way to cut off Grant's line of march.

The first shock took place 'twixt War-ren's corps and

VIII.--BAT-TLE OF THE WIL-DER-NESS.

Ew-ell's corps on the Or-ange turn-pike near the Old Wil der-ness Inn, where a fierce fight raged mid the scrub-oaks and low pines whose roots ran on top of the ground. It was Lee's plan to crush Grant at the start.

At length some of Sedg-wick's corps came up to the aid of War-ren's men; and Han-cock came up on the left and fought with Hill who had in the mean-time made his way to Ew-ell's right.

SKIR-MISH-ING IN THE WIL-DER-NESS.

Till eight o'clock the bat-tle raged in Hill's front. Night brought it to an end. Grant made up his mind to charge with all the lines by dawn of the next day. But the same plan was in Lee's mind, and at day-light on the 5th of May he made an on-set on Sedg-wick. Then the roll of the drum, and the gleam of the guns on Han-cock's front told that the line was on the march there. A hard fight took place, and Han-cock's corps drove back the corps of Hill's for more than a mile

By this time fresh troops had brought fresh strength to both sides. Long-street came up to the aid of Hill; and Burn-side to help War-ren and Han-cock. All through the day it was a dead-lock fight, in which the loss was great on both sides. The woods took fire, and the blaze swept close up to the breast-works, which were of wood, and soon a mass of flames. Red hot tongues of fire leaped round the legs of the men as they fought. The heat and smoke drove some of Han-cock's men from a point they had held. This made a break in the line. The foe rush up and plant their flags on the breast-works, but do not stay long. Car-roll, with Bir-ney's corps, puts them to route, and thus they fight, to and fro, on this strange field.

Lee knew the ground. He was at home there. But it was new to Grant and his men. They did not know where the roads were, nor to what place they led. Yet in spite of this they made out to keep Lee back, and drove him at last as far as Spott-syl-va-ni-a. This was on the 6th of May, and the next day when scouts were sent out they found the gray coats as thick as the blue on the field that for three days had been the scene of such a hard fight. There were no signs of life. Some had been shot dead, and those who had met with wounds were choked by the smoke and flames that raged around them.

On the night of the 7th Grant and Meade, with their aides-de-camp, took up their line of march to Rich-mond. The troops had thought they would have to turn back and cross the Rap-i-dan, and this did not please them. The word went from man to man that Grant had his face set to-ward Rich-mond. Stiff and sore as they were and spite of their wounds they made the Wil-der-ness ring with cheers.

They could not see the face of their chief. Most of them did not know him at all. But this move gave them cheer; for they knew that he had not lost hope, and would lead them on to win the prize for which they fought, and bring peace to the land.

So long and loud were their shouts that the Rebs who were quite near, thought it was a night at-tack, and came out to the front, and the noise of their guns chimed in with the cheers that Han-cock's men gave to Grant.

Spott-syl-va-ni-a lay 'twixt the Po and the Ny, two small streams that were but three or four miles a-part. A thick growth of woods was on their banks, and a stretch of swamp-land in front. Hills and dales were all round, and at the south a range of hills, on the crest of which were earth-works with great trees laid in front in such a way as to screen them from the foe. You will see by this in what a strong-hold Lee and his troops were, and how hard a task it would be for Grant to drive them out. Spott-syl-va-ni-a was right in Grant's path, and if he got to Rich-mond at all, he would have to turn Lee's lines, or to hem him in so that he would have to give up the fight.

WOUND-ED LEAV-ING THE BAT-TLE OF THE WIL-DER-NESS

Lee was a brave man, and a great chief. The South had great faith in him. He had a deep hold on their hearts. Should he fail them, their cause would in deed be lost. The eyes of the whole North and South were turned to this place, where these two men stood, as it were, face to face.

For ten days Grant sought in vain to pierce or take Lee's strong-hold. It was from Spott-syl-va-ni-a that Grant sent this word that has won such fame: "*I pro-pose to fight it out on this line, if it takes all Sum-mer.*

Now and then a point was won, and then lost. Right and left the fight went on till the woods were set on fire and Grant's troops had to fall back.

On the night of the 11th of May the 2nd corps were brought as near as they could get to the earth-works they were to storm, and at dawn of the next day with cheers and shouts they went up the steep, tore down the trees, and with a dash swept in on the foe. Here they had a hand-to-hand fight; took a large part of Ew-ell's corps, and drove the rest of them for the space of half a mile. Here they found a new line of breast-works. Lee sent a large force to take the lost ground, and Hancock's men had to make their way back to the line of works they had first seized. There Grant's troops held their own, and day by day made such fierce at-tacks on Lee that the ground was strewn with the dead; some in blue and some in gray.

"Push on—push hard," said Grant, who was bound not to let go when he had a good grip. And push on they did, with a good will and a strong will till Lee had to fall back and leave the field.

Brave men fought on both sides at the Wil-der-ness and at Spott-syl-va-ni-a. Grant lost 13,601 men, Lee's loss is not known, but is thought to have been full as great.

CHAPTER X.

BY THE LEFT-FLANK.

SHER-I-DAN, who led the troops that were on horseback, had made a raid on Lee's lines, put Stu-art to flight, and then made a dash on the out-works of Richmond. In the vale of the Shen-an-do-ah, Si-gel had fought, but shown no skill, and Hun-ter was sent to take his place. On the line of the James, But-ler had had a hard fight with Beau-re-gard, in which he met with great loss and had to draw back to a place known as Ber-mu-da Hun-dred, whence he sent troops to Grant, while Beau-re-gard sent troops to Lee.

The foes next met at Chick-a-hom-i-ny, a wide marsh, where a host of boys in blue had found their graves when they were in camp there the first two years of the war.

Thick pine woods and a dense growth of shrubs and of dwarf trees hedge in the foe. The hills are not high, but here and there is a deep gorge which serves to keep at bay the boys in blue.

Sharp fights took place on the road as Grant's men

DEATH OF GEN-ER-AL SEDG-WICK.

came up from Spott-syl-va-ni-a. They had to cross the North An-na, and the Pa-mun-key. Sher-i-dan was sent to find out where Lee was. Gregg's corps was with him. They came on a troop of horse and of men, at a place near Me-chan-ics-ville. Here a sharp fight took place, and both sides held their own. Late in the day Cus-ter came up, and with the aid of Gregg's corps made a fierce at-tack, drove the Rebs out of their line of works, and forced them to leave their dead on the field.

On the 31st of May, Sher-i-dan—of whose brave deeds I am sure you will like to read—had got as far as Old Cold Har-bor, where he found a force of men on horse and on foot, back of breast-works of logs and rails. He had a hard fight, but at last drove the foe from the place. But they soon came back, and with such a large force, that Sher-i-dan thought that he could not hold the prize. But ere he could move out, he was met by word from Grant to hold the place at all risks. So he went to work to guard the place—and to make

FORD-ING THE NORTH AN-NA.

it as strong as he could—and to wait for the at-tack which they heard the foe plan to make the next morn.

At day-light on the 1st of June, the Rebs in front of Sher-i-dan charge on the works he has won. He lets them come up quite close, and then pours on them such a fire that they fall back in great haste. Once more they strive to take the place, but Sher-i-dan holds fast. The Sixth corps, which Grant had sent to his aid, should have been at Cold Har-bor at day-light, but the road was long, and it was nine o'clock ere they came in sight.

For four hours Sher-i-dan had kept up the fight though the foe had far more men than he had, and as soon as the Sixth corps came to help him, Old Cold Har-bor was lost to Lee.

Mean-while Lee kept his troops on a line with

Grant's, and at each fresh move on his part met him with a fierce fire of shot and shell.

A mile and a half west of Old Cold Har-bor, on the road to Rich-mond, is a long, low hill that ends in a swamp, at the south side near the Chick-a-hom-i-ny On the north side a deep gorge here and there breaks the slope. The right flank of Lee's troops was on the crest of this ridge. There was no need for them to throw up earth-works, or to do the least thing to make their strong-hold safe. They were shut in on all sides, and those who would dare to come near them would meet the full force of their guns.

BOMB PROOFS AT COLD HAR-BOR.

At half-past four a.m., on the 3rd of June, the line on the left—the 6th, the 18th, and the 2nd corps, set out to break Lee's line. But though they fought hard all day, they did not make much head-way.

When Grant found that he could not get to Rich-mond by this route, he made up his mind to cross the James and lay siege to Pe-ters-burg, which you will see

RAIL TIE BAR-RI-CADE.

by the map is just south of, and right on a line with, Rich-mond.

All the rail-roads that led to Rich-mond were in the hands of the foe; a large fleet of gun-boats and rams were in front of the town; and the bed of the James was full of strange craft that would blow up all boats which came up the stream. From Dru-ry's Bluff it winds its way in great curves to Cit-y Point, where it is more than half a mile wide. There was but one point where Grant could cross the James, and that was a long way from Cold Har-bor. His troops would have to march at least three-score miles, and be in fear all the time, that the foe might rush out on them and stop their course.

Lee was on the watch all the time, and the boys in blue could not make the least move that was not seen by him. But he was not quite so bold as Grant, and did not guess what his plans were.

It was on the night of the 12th of June that the Ar-my of the Po-to-mac took up its line of march. In the dark they had to plough their way through swamps, climb the great drift-logs, and cross the Chick-a-hom-i-ny at Long Bridge. There was no bridge there, so they had to make use of the limbs of the trees that hung down o'er the stream, and in this way got a foot-hold on the south bank. Then a bridge of boats was laid so that the men on foot and on horse-back could cross with speed, and soon the whole force

TAV-ERN AT COLD HAR-BOR.

was on its way to the James by the roads that led through White Oak Swamp. A sharp fight took place at Riddle's shop.

The North had a fleet of gun-boats to guard the James from its mouth to Ber-mu-da Hun-dred but Grant did not think they could hold the stream. So on the night of the 13th he sent word to But-ler to fill a lot of boats with stone, and sink them so that no boats from Rich-mond could come down and seize the stores, or check the march of the boys in blue. But-ler had had a lot

THE CHICK-A-HOM-I-NY SWAMPS.

of boats filled with stone, as he thought there might be need of them, but it was not his place to put them in the stream till his chief told him to do so. When the word came no time was lost.

Grant sent word to Lin-coln that his plan was to reach Pe-ters-burg, where he could bring troops in front of the town with more speed than Lee could. "I think your plan a good one," Lin-coln wrote back. "You are sure to win. God bless you all."

But there was a great hue and cry at the North when they found out that Grant was on the way to Pe-ters-burg and not to Rich-mond. They did not know, as he did, that to crush Lee was to crush the South. At this time there was but a small force of men on guard in Pe-ters-burg. Beau-re-gard's force was in front of Ber-mu-da Hun-dred. Lee and his troops were north of the James. By a quick and prompt at-tack Grant was in hopes to take the town.

One who was with him tells of the scene on the banks of the James: "At Wil-cox's Land-ing, where the troops were to cross, the stream was less than half a mile wide. In the dark hours of the night of June 14th the bridge

of boats was built, and at mid-night the men took up their march, with the great field guns, and by day-light the whole of the Second corps was safe on the south bank of the stream. It took all that day for the Ar-my of the Po-to-mac to cross the James. The banks were lined with troops. On the great bridge of boats was a stream of men on foot and on horse-back—of great guns on wheels, and of huge carts full of the tools of war. The guns shone bright in the light of the sun. The flags were gay. To and fro went the aides-de-camp on horse-back. On one side were the gun-boats. Down the stream a fleet was in sight with more troops on board; and the roar of Wil-son's and War-ren's guns were heard as they kept guard at the rear."

The troops have to pass through woods where there are no roads, and through low swamp-lands where the wheels sink deep in the mire. Still they press on, and by day-break the head of the line comes up with the out-guards of the foe. At six o'clock, as they near the Cit-y Point road, they are met by a fire of guns from a fort on Bay-lor's farm, six miles from Pe-ters-burg. Here there was a sharp fight, but at the end of two hours the Rebs were put to flight, and by noon Grant's whole force was in front of Pe-ters-burg.

A RAM-ON THE JAMES RIV-ER.

The men could move but a few rods at a time ere they came in range of the guns of the foe Then they would have to lie down and wait for the next chance. Soon they would rise, push on a few rods, and then lie down once more. This was slow work, of course, and it was half-past one when they came to the ground from which the first at-tack was to be made. Here they lay for five long hours, while the great guns from the forts kept up their roar and sent their shells right at them. This was a great strain on the nerves of the men.

W. F. Smith was at the head of the boys in blue, and at the end of the five hours he sent out more than half his troops to charge on the works on the Cit-y Point and Prince George Court-house roads. They were met by a sharp fire, but the troops forced their way in to the works which were on the crest of a deep wild gorge. Kid-doo's black troops were the first to gain the hill. The foe, borne down in front and flank, gave way, and

CROSS-ING THE JAMES RIV-ER ON PON-TOON BRIDG-ES.

at dusk Smith had seized the whole line of the out-works, two and a half miles long, with a lot of men and guns. Pe-ters-burg was in his grasp. There was no force 'twixt him and the Ap-po-mat-tox, but a part of the corps, led by Gen-er-al Wise, and the town troops, made up of old men and boys.

Han-cock, Bir-ney, and Gib-bon were soon on their way to aid Smith, who it was thought would push to the front, and seize Pe-ters-burg. But he was a slow man, and did not like to take the risk. He thought it best to wait till the next day.

Grant was at Cit-y Point so as to be near But-ler and Meade, and it was near day-light, on the 16th, when he heard that Smith was at a stand-still. He rode out at once to Pe-ters-burg. But by this time Lee was on the

CHARGE AT PE-TERS-BURG.—FIRST DAY.

move, and Beau-re-gard had sent word to Rich-mond that he must have more troops or he could not hold both Pe-ters-burg and the lines in front of But-ler. The prize that might have been won by Smith's corps at small cost, would now be hard to take.

The town was in charge, not of old men and boys, but of strong men, full of skill, some of whom had been to West Point to learn the art of war.

Grant at once brought his force up to the front as he meant to storm the town at six o'clock that night.

Meade was put in charge of all the troops in front of Pe-ters-burg. At the first charge Han-cock drove the foe back, and as it was a fine moon-light night the fight was kept up, and the foe tried hard to get back the ground they had lost. But in vain.

For two days more the fight went on. Now the Ninth corps won a strong-hold, and then lost it. Fresh troops were sent to their aid, but they could not get back what they had lost. Wright did not think they could hold the works if they should seize them. Pe-ters-burg was still in the hands of Lee.

Meade tried his best to urge his men on. "Get the best line you can," he said, "and make up your minds to hold it."

At ten o'clock on the night of the 18th, Grant said to Meade, "All has been done that could be done. Now we will rest the men, and use the spade—till a new vein can be struck."

Then Grant went to work to hem in Pe-ters-burg, as he did Vicks-burg, to seize all the rail-roads, and put the town in a state of siege. All this would take time, but the men were worn out and had need of rest, and it was well to wait.

On the 21st of June, Lin-coln rode out to the front

of both Meade's and But-ler's lines. On his way back he had to pass through the black troops who had fought so well in the first charge on Pe-ters-burg. They crowd 'round him with tears in their eyes. They greet him

LIN-COLN THE BLACK MAN'S FRIEND.

with cheers and cries of joy. He is their friend. These men were slaves. He set them free. They laugh, they cry. They press up to him to shake or kiss his hand, to touch his clothes, or the horse on which he rode. It was a sight to move strong men.

Lin-coln rode by the black men with his hat off, too full of tears (not of grief, but of joy) to trust him-self to speak.

CHAPTER XI.

THE SIEGE OF PE-TERS-BURG.

ON the night of the 21st of June, the 2nd and 6th corps were in front of a large force of the foe.

On the 22nd, Bir-ney, who had charge of the 2nd corps was sent to the left, where he could cross the Wel-don road and then get round to the Ap-po-mat-tox, a stream which runs north of the town. Wright was sent to the left, not by the same road as Bir-ney, and soon found some of the foe with whom he had a sharp fight. Bar-low had been sent to add strength to Bir-ney's line, and a part of Hill's corps came in the gap 'twixt him and Wright, and put his men to rout. At the same time Gib-bon, who was on Bir-ney's right, had a hot fight with the foe who drove his men back with the loss of four of their guns.

This took place late in the day. There was no great gain to North or South, and in the night Lee fell back to his works.

On the 20th word came from Ab-er-crom-bie, who had been left at White House, that a large force of the

Rebs had made an at-tack on him. Grant told him to hold out at all risks for Sher-i-dan was at hand

Beau-re-gard and Lee were as keen and as full of craft as Grant and Meade. Troops had been sent at once to stop Sher-i-dan on the rail-road, and then to the White House, so that he could not cross the Pa-mun-key. Breck-en-ridge and Ear-ly were first sent to Gor-dons-ville, and then to Lynch-burg, to meet and chase Hun-ter, whom Grant had sent to West Vir-gin-i-a, and who was now on his way back to the main line.

On the 21st, But-ler threw a bridge of boats a-cross the James, and made his way to Deep Bot-tom, ten miles from Rich-mond, on the north side. This was done to get a foot-hold on the north bank of the stream, and to put Lee in doubt as to Grant's plans. At the same time Wil-son went on his raid to seize all the rail-roads he could lay hands on, and the news came in that White House was safe, for Sher-i-dan was there.

White House had been the base where all the stores were kept for use in the Ar-my of the Po-to-mac. When Sher-i-dan came to this place he found a note from Grant that told him to leave the place, move the teams, and cross the Chick-a-hom-i-ny at Jones's bridge.

On the 24th he was on his way.

To reach the bridge of boats at Deep Bot-tom where he could cross the James, he would have to march as far as Charles Cit-y Court-house, and then by Har-ri-son's Land-ing and Mal-vern Hill, where the foe were. The train that Sher-i-dan had charge of was ten miles long.

As Tor-bert's corps went out on the Court-house road they fell in with the foe, who drove them so they had to cross Her-ring creek on the road to West-o-ver church. As soon as Sher-i-dan heard of this, he cried "Halt!" and the whole train came to a stand-still. Then he sent word to Tor-bert to push to the front and meet the foe, while Gregg, who was on the right flank of the trains, and who had met the foe on that side, was to hold fast till all the carts could pass the Court-house. Then the train moved on, and on the 26th of June was safe at the north of the James, and not a horse or cart was lost.

At St. Ma-ry's church Gregg had a hard fight with Hamp-ton, which was kept up till dark, and from which he had to fall back, though with no great loss.

For some days the heat

was so great that the men had no strength to fight. There was no rain, and clouds of dust rose thick on the air. The troops were in need of rest, and Grant had a chance to look round and work out the plan he had had in his mind for some time.

Sher-man was in the heart of Geor-gi-a, and his wants must be seen to. Troops must be sent to Sher-i-dan. Wil-son might need help. Hun-ter, as soon as he could get out of the net in which he was caught, was to start for Char-lottes-ville, to tear up the road at that place.

On the 28th of June Meade sent word to Grant that a large force of the Rebs on horse-back had been seen to pass to the left and the rear on the Wel-don road. It was thought their plan was to come in 'twixt Sher-i-dan and Wil-son. Wil-son had not been heard from for some time, and it was not known just where he was. On the 22nd of June he had set out from Prince George Court-house, with a large force of men.

Kautz had the lead and went at once to Ream's, where he broke up the road and the house that stood there. Thence by Din-wid-die Court-house to the south side road. Here the rear of the line was set on by a troop of horse—W. F. Lee's corps—but no great fight took place.

Kautz was at Ford's by four p.m., and here he seized cars, burnt the house, the tanks, and the cross-ties, and tore up the rails for miles and miles, while Wil-son's own corps tore up and burnt the rails from Six-teen-mile Turn-out to Ford's.

DE-STROY-ING A RAIL-ROAD.

On the 23rd Kautz came to the point where the Dan-ville and South-side roads cross. It was thought the South would fight hard to keep this road, as it was worth a great deal to them. Kautz soon drove back the force that was there, and set his men to burn the house and the tanks, and to tear up the roads.

They would lay fence-rails length-wise on the road and set fire to them. This would make the steel rails warp and swell and so spoil the ties that both roads were of no use.

Wil-son came up to aid in this work, and at Not-to-way Court-house had a sharp fight with W. F. Lee, who got in 'twixt him and Kautz. Wil-son at last drove back the foe that sought to stop him, and came up with Kautz on the Dan-ville road, with the loss of three-score and ten men.

On the 25th the whole force, with Kautz still in the van, came to Ro-an-oke, where there was a bridge for the Dan-ville rail-road to cross the Staun-ton. They at once set out to burn the north end of the bridge. But the Rebs had six guns on the south bank, four lines of pits and a small force from Dan-ville.

Wil-son saw that it would cost too much to take the bridge. The Rebs were close in the rear; the Staun-ton was too deep to ford; he had no bridge boats; and so he made up his mind to turn back. This he did in the night, by a road that ran south-east by the bank of the stream, and less than half a mile from the guns of the foe. For the next two days they march due east, and as they near Sto-ny Creek, on the Wel-don road, they

CAV-AL-RY FIGHT AT REAM'S STA-TION.

learn that Hamp-ton and W. F. Lee are there in wait for them.

Here a fierce fight takes place and Wil-son's troops are put to rout. Some of them take to the woods. Wil-son re-forms his lines and moves on to Ream's. The foe are close at his rear, and at Sto-ny Creek they make a hard push to get up to him. But though the bridge is bad, and the stream too deep to ford, and the shot falls thick and fast round their heads, they make out to cross, and with great haste press on to the Not-to-way, which they reach late at night. At dawn, on the 30th they reach Jar-rott's on the Wel-don rail-way. Wil-son learns that a force has left Sto-ny Creek to stop him on the Je-ru-sa-lem road. On he goes with haste, and is soon at Black-wa-ter, where he finds the bridge gone, and the stream too deep to ford. He at once sets his men to work to re-build the bridge, which is soon fit to cross. But as the wood has been just burnt it gives way while the troops are on it, and has to be built up once more. Twice this takes place, and then the men cut great beams from the woods, put the planks on them, and soon the troops cross the stream. Then the bridge is burnt, and none too soon, for the foe are close in the rear, and when they come to the stream they find the bridge gone, and so give up the chase.

Wil-son, now that he was safe, let his troops rest for a few hours, and then moved to Cab-in Point, on the James, where he went in camp. On the 2nd of July he was at Light House Point. He had been gone on his raid ten days and a half, had had a long march; had been in four hard fights; and had torn up miles and miles of rail-roads. At no place did the troops rest more than six hours, and in the last four days did not halt for more than four hours at a time.

Hun-ter was on the way to Lynch-burg, and had had

more than one fight with Ear-ly, who kept close on his track.

On the 3rd of Ju-ly, Breck-en-ridge was sent out by Rob-ert E. Lee to march on Mar-tins-burg, while a large force went to the east to Lee-town, to check the move that Si-gel would have to make. As soon as Breck-en-ridge drew near, Si-gel left Mar-tins-burg, met the van-guard of the foe at Lee-town, drove it back, and went at once to Ma-ry-land Heights, the hills that look down on Har-per's Fer-ry.

The Rebs gave chase on the 4th, and on that day the boys in blue left Har-per's Fer-ry, burnt the rail-roads and bridge of boats, which they had made use of to cross the Po-to-mac at this point, and put all their strength on the Heights. It was a strong-hold in-deed. The hills were high and steep, and on the crest were guns of great size, and so the town at their feet was safe from the foe

Ear-ly had to fall back as far as Shep-herds-town, and cross the stream at that point, and as he found he could not move Si-gel, he took his march through the gaps in the hills north of the Heights, and made his stand at Fred-er-ick, on the Mon-o-ca-cy. From this place he sent troops to tear up the rail-road 'twixt Bal-ti-more and Wash-ing-ton.

This bold act set the whole North on fire. It was meant to scare them, and to make Grant let go his hold. Ear-ly went as far as Rock-ville creek, but Grant soon had troops from east and west on his path, and they drove him back as far as Stras-burg. Grant felt that these raids in Ma-ry-land must be put a stop to at once, and as Wright could not keep up with Ear-ly or do him harm, he sent for him and the Sixth corps to come back as soon as they could to the lines in front of Pe-ters-burg.

But Hun-ter had sent word to Lin-coln that if he was to hold the rail-road and keep back Ear-ly he must have Wright to help him. This word was sent to Grant, and though it would thwart his plans, he sent word back that it would suit him best to have a smash up of the roads round Gor-dons-ville and Char-lottes-ville. "If Wright and Hun-ter can do this job, let them do it."

One mile from Pe-ters-burg, in a straight line, was a deep gorge, which some of the troops near there thought would be a good place to start a mine to blow up the town. So they went to work with spade and pick, all the tools they had, and by the last of Ju-ly the mine was dug and the charge was laid.

At half-past three on the morn of the 30th, Burn-side

PICK-ETS TRA-DING BE-TWEEN THE LINES.

was to spring the mine, move his lines with speed up through the breach, seize the crest of the hill in the rear, and make a strong-hold of that place. Ord was to come up on his right, War-ren on his left, and all the plans were laid so that it would turn out well. Meade was in charge of all the troops.

As the hour drew near Burn-side said that as the white troops were in need of rest, the black troops ought to take the lead in the pass. They were fresh, and had done no work in the mine, while some of the white men were quite worn out. Meade did not like this plan. The black troops had done well when put on guard, but they did not know how to fight. It was a new thing to them, but they did the best they could. Burn-side thought his way was the right one, and so lots were drawn to see which of the three—Burn-side, War-ren, or Led-lie—should take the lead. The lot fell on Led-lie, who was at the head of the black troops.

BOMB PROOFS AT PE-TERS-BURG

On the night of the 30th of July the match was lit, but the mine was not sprung. There was some thing wrong. Two brave men, Lieu-ten-ant Dough-ty and Ser-geant (*sar-jent*) Rees, of the 48th Penn-syl-va-ni-a went in the mine, and found the fuse had burnt out. It took them an hour to fix it. Then they lit the match, got out safe, and soon there was a shock like an earth-quake, and up in the air went guns, men, and huge blocks of clay, and when the smoke and dust went off there was a great chasm in the place where the Rebs had had their fort.

EX-PLO-SION OF MINE AT PE-TERS-BURG.

Led-lie did not move his troops up as he should have done, and Meade sent word to Burn-side to push his troops to the crest of the hill. But there was a snarl of

MOR-TAR BAT-TE-RY.

some sort—and this gave the Rebs time to get on their feet.

Mean-while Meade was in a state of fear lest this chance should be lost, and at six o'clock he sent this word to Burn-side: "There is no line in the rear of the Rebs. None of their troops have come back from the James. Our chance is now. Push your men to the front at all risks—white and black. Lose no time, but rush for the crest."

The black troops went up the slope as bold as could be, and tried to take the hill. But the fire from the Rebs broke up their ranks, and they fled in wild haste to the rear. Not a few of the white troops went with them in their flight, but the rest tried to fight their way through the pass.

But the Rebs had brought up troops on all sides, and from the crest in front, and from the chasms and lines on the flanks they sent a storm of shot and shell in-to the hole. At last Grant rode out to the front, got off his horse, and though shot and shell went by him, made his way to where Burn-side stood. He saw that there was no chance for the Yanks. The Rebs had it all their own way, and it was no use to waste more lives. So the troops were drawn from the mine, and the work that was done there had been all in vain. It was a great blow to Grant, but he did not lose heart or hope.

On the 7th of Au-gust, Grant put Sher-i-dan in charge of all the troops that were in Wash-ing-ton. He would make warm work for Ear-ly, and tease him to death.

Phil. Sher-i-dan at this time was not quite two-score. He was short and thick-set, had a large head, and wore his hair cut close. His face was red, and his eyes black. Though fond of fun, he could look stern when there was need, and was a man to love, to fear, and to trust. His plans were all well-laid. He knew what risks he took, and when it was wise not to take them. He would dash here and there through the fight with his sword drawn, and with an air that gave cheer and strength to his men. It might be said that he put life in them; for it is told that when one of his men was shot in the fight at Five Forks, Sher-i-dan cried out "There's no harm done."

and the man went on with a ball in his brain till he fell dead on the field.

The time had come for a grand move on three points. The lines were to be drawn in so as to crush the foe. On the 10th of Au-gust, Sher-i-dan set out to meet Ear-ly, and drove him back as far as Stras-burg. Sher-i-dan went in camp on the heights north of the town, on Ce-dar creek. At this point he got word from Grant that a large force had gone from Rich-mond to Ear-ly, and that he would have to watch each move that was made, and give chase at once if Ear-ly should turn to the north. He was to do all the harm that he could to crops and to rail-roads, to seize all the live-stock, and leave no wheat or hay for the Rebs to use. This had to be done so that the foe would not make raids on the free States. The free States were those where no slaves were kept.

On the night of the 15th of Sep-tem-ber, Sher-i-dan found out that a part of Ear-ly's force, led by An-der-son, was on the move through Win-ches-ter, on the way to Front Roy-al. Sher-i-dan had a mind to meet them at New-town, in the rear of Win-ches-ter, but thought it best to wait till he could have a talk with Grant. On the 17th, Ear-ly went to Mar-tins-burg with some of his men, to tear up the rail-road, and left the rest of his force in front of Win-ches-ter. So Sher-i-dan made a change in his plans and left Ber-ry-ville, where he had been for some days. At Mar-tins-burg, Ear-ly found out that Grant had been with Sher-i-dan, and as he thought some great move was to be made in front of Pe-ters-burg, he at once came back. At day-light on the 19th there was one corps of the Rebs in front of Sher-i-dan; one five miles to the north; and one quite close at hand; and he must fight them all.

The at-tack was made in fine style. The boys in gray drove back the boys in blue. Then they in turn had to give way. Sher-i-dan sent Crook to find out the left of the line of the Rebs, and to strike it in flank or rear, and to break it up, while he made a left half-wheel on the main line to aid them. Crook went up with a dash, and drove the Rebs from their place. Wil-son made a push to the left to gain the roads that led south from Win-ches-ter, while Tor-bert made a charge in front with the troops that were left.

The fear that they might be shut in on all sides broke up the lines of the foe, whom Sher-i-dan sent with a whirl through Win-ches-ter. In the night, Ear-ly fell back as far as New-town, and next day to Fish-er's Hill,

—T V -R H–

four miles south of Stras-burg, with Sher-i-dan in full chase.

In this fight both Sher-i-dan and Ear-ly lost 4,500 men.

At Fish-er's Hill the Rebs had put up breast-works the whole length of the low-land, here three miles and a half wide. On the night of Sep-tem-ber 20th Sher-i-dan took his stand on the heights of Stras-burg. Crook lay hid in the dense woods. Tor-bert was sent to the left to stop the Rebs at New-mar-ket, a score of miles back of Ear-ly.

Ere day-light on the 22nd the fight took place. The 6th and 19th corps came up in front, while Rick-ett's corps and Av-er-ill's troop of horse-men came up with a great show on the left. Just as the Rebs had got to work, and the fire of the guns was fierce on both sides, Crook burst from the woods on the hill-side, struck the Rebs in flank and rear, and swept down back of their breast-works. Sher-i-dan's main line then took part in the fight, seized the works and put the foe to rout. It was dark ere the fight came to an end, but the Rebs kept up their flight through Wood-stock, and as far as a gorge in the Blue Ridge.

Sher-i-dan gave chase all through the night, but made a halt at Wood-stock to rest and feed his men.

On the 23rd he drove the foe to Mount Jack-son, and on the 24th to a point six miles from New-mar-ket. Had Tor-bert been there to check the flight of the Rebs, the whole of Ear-ly's force would have met its doom. But Tor-bert had had hard work to get through a gorge, and fear lent wings to the feet of those who fled for their lives. On the 25th, Ear-ly fell back as far as Brown's Gap, and left the vale of Vir-gin-i-a in Sher-i-dan's hands.

CHAPTER XII.

THE MARCH TO THE SEA.

SHER-I-DAN'S good luck gave great joy to Grant, as well as to the whole North. Grant was quick to praise him and to thank him for what he had done, and it was this trait of the great chief's that made his men so fond of him.

Now we will leave the Ar-my on the James for a while, and take a look at Sher-man who was at the head of the Ar-my of the Ten-nes-see. He had a great scheme in his mind. Hood was Lee's right hand man at this point.

Sher-man had to guard a long line of rail-road, from Nash-ville to At-lan-ta, and the need of troops there took from the strength of his force. Mo-bile and At-lan-ta were safe.

At this time, to cheer the hearts of the Rebs, Jeff Da-vis came from Rich-mond to the camp of Hood, and all on the road, to tell them of new plans that had been made which were sure to crush the North.

"Be of good cheer," he said, "for in a short time you

will turn home-ward, and your feet will press the soil of Ten-nes-see." The new plans were put in print, and so Sher-man knew, of course, just what to do.

On the 29th of Sep-tem-ber, Hood and his troops cross the Chat-ta-hoo-chee, and on this day Grant made a move in front of Rich-mond so that Lee would not keep too close a watch on Sher-man. Sher-man gave chase to Hood, who he knew was on the way to Al-la-too-na, where the food was stored to feed the boys in blue. This would be a great prize. From hill-top to hill-top flags were sent that would tell Corse, who was at Rome, to haste at once to Al-la-too-na. Sher-man did not reach Ken-e-saw till the 5th of Oc-to-ber, and by this time the Rebs had struck the rail-road, and the whole line at his feet for miles and miles bore marks of the fires. He could see the smoke of the fight, and hear the roar of the big guns a score of miles a-way.

He at once told the 23rd corps to march due west, to burn bush or to set a house on fire to mark the head of the line, and come in 'twixt Hood and the Rebs in force at Al-la-too-na.

Not a word since day-light had been heard from Gen er-al Corse; but as Sher-man stood on Ken-e-saw Mount he caught sight through a gap, of the tell-tale flag, on which was C. R. S. E. H. E. R. He made sense out of it at once. "Corse is here." This was the first that Sher-man knew that Corse had got the word from him, and he had less fear for Al-la-too-na. By two o'clock in the day the smoke grew less and less, and at four the fight came to an end. The tell-tale flag let Sher-man know that Hood was sent back, and that Corse had a bad wound.

HOLD THE FORT FLAG SIG-NAL.

He was "short a cheek bone and an ear," but still full of fight.

On the 10th of Oc-to-ber Hood was at Rome, and Sher-man's whole force gave chase as far as Kings-ton. When they came to the place they found that Hood had fled. On the 12th the Rebs were at Re-sa-ca. Hood bade those on guard there give up the post, or they would take it by storm.

"If you want it, come and take it," was the word sent back.

This Hood did not do, but kept on his march to the north and tore up all the rail-ways on his route.

For the first eight days of Oc-to-ber Sher-man had sent no word to Grant, but on the ninth he made known to him his plan to march to the sea-coast. "I can make the march," he wrote, "and make Geor-gi-a howl."

Grant at first did not like to have Sher-man turn his back on the foe. He thought it might be best to fight Hood, and then set out on the march. Sher-man was sure that Hood would chase him. Grant was as sure that the Rebs would go north. Grant had no force to send to meet him at Sa-van-nah. Still Sher-man had a mind to move to the sea. It was a bold scheme.

It was not till the 15th of No-vem-ber that Sher-man set out on his great march to the sea-coast. His troops were made up of four corps. Gen-er-al How-ard had charge of the right wing. Gen-er-al Slo-cum of the left. How-ard with the horse-men went to the south-east, while Slo-cum led off to the east, by way of De-ca-tur and Mad-i-son. Mil-ledge-ville was the point they were to strike, and it would take them a week to reach that place.

They took no tents. They made their beds of pine boughs. They fed off the land, and the farms on their route, and at night the sky was red with the fires they lit to burn the rail-road ties. They would march from ten to a score of miles each day. The troops were kept in good health, and the live-stock were well fed, and the deeds that we would call crimes in times of peace, were not thought to be such in war times.

The Rebs thought that Sher-man meant to march on Au-gus-ta, or Ma-con, and at once went to work to add to the strength of each place, and to guard well the stores there.

On the 22nd the right and left wing met the main line at Mil-ledge-ville. The chief men of the State, those who made the laws, fled from the place; but the towns-folks staid in their homes. The Rebs came out of Ma-con, but the boys in blue drove them back and kept on to the O-co-nee, where once more they fell in with the foe, who tried to drive them back in turn. But a bridge of boats is soon laid, and the right wing cross the stream, and are safe from harm for a while.

The march was laid out for each day; each wing was

told which route to take, and where they were to camp at noon and at night, and on they went with brave hearts to the goal they sought to win. As they came near San-ders-ville the Rebs set fire to the stacks of grain that stood in the fields. Sher-man at once made it known to those who dwelt in and near that place, that if they burnt food or hay on his route he would make a clean sweep of the whole land. This put a stop to the waste, and the troops went on, tore up the rail-roads, and lived on the fat of the land.

They did not fare so well as they drew near the coast, where the ground was bare, and the soil poor. But though corn and grass were scarce, there were rice fields close at hand, and on this grain both men and beasts were fed.

By the 8th of De-cem-ber the van reach Poo-ler's station, eight miles from Sa-van-nah. Sher-man rode forth to spy out the land, and soon came to a dense wood. He got off his horse, and found a space through which he could see the out-works of Sa-van-nah, at least half a mile a-way. Here was a wide ditch, there a swamp or a creek. The whole land round Sa-van-nah was a great salt marsh—hard to cross—and the out-works were so strong that Sher-man felt that a siege was close at hand.

The fleet, with the Stars and Stripes at mast-head, lay in Ty-bee, Os-sa-baw, and Was-saw sounds. He must let them know where he was, so that they could aid him in this strait. In the mean-time he shut in the town on the north and west—Slo-cum on the left, and How-ard on the right—so that no stores could reach Sa-van-nah by these routes.

On the 13th of De-cem-ber, Sher-man sent out a corps of men in charge of Brig-a-dier Gen-er-al Ha-zen. They were to march down the west bank of the O-gee-chee, and take Fort McAl-lis-ter by storm. It was a strong fort, and in it was a large force of men and guns—great guns that could send huge balls, and fire at a long range.

A GREAT GUN.

Ha-zen put some of his men where they could see and yet not be seen. The trunks of trees hid them, and they could pick off the men at the guns in the fort if they dared to show their heads. The rest of the troops went up the hill in three lines, and met at the same time on the wall at the top, and drove the Rebs to the bomb-proofs, where a hand-to-hand fight took place. This was kept up till the last Reb gave way, and Fort McAl-lis-ter was won.

For two days Sher-man's troops had been on the look-out, from trees and hill-tops, for some sign of the fleet. But not a flag was to be seen. At last Sher-man, who kept a watch on each move that Ha-zen made, saw a long way off, where the sky bent down to the sea, some-thing that was like the smoke-pipe of a steam-ship. It comes fast! It draws near! A flag goes up—and all goes well!

As soon as the Stars and Stripes were seen on the wall, Sher-man went to the fort, found a skiff near at hand, and with a crew of men who laid down their guns to take up the oars, was soon on his way down the stream. Night had set in, but six miles from the fort he saw a light. It was the ship that led the fleet, and Sher-man was soon on board.

It was just one month since he had left At-lan-ta. The march to the sea was made, and the whole land rang with shouts and cheers. The end drew near. Thom-as had whipped Hood, and the names of Sher-man and Thom-as were in all men's mouths.

CHAPTER XIII.

THE FIGHT AT CE-DAR CREEK.

Now we must go back to see what has been done by the Ar-my on the James. Ere the dawn of day on the 29th of Sep-tem-ber But-ler made a move from Deep Bot-tom, which was but ten miles from Rich-mond. Ord led the 18th corps by the Va-ri-na road. Bir-ney the 10th corps, by the New-mar-ket road. Kautz, with the men on horse-back, took the Dar-by-town road on the right of the troops on foot. They took Fort Har-ri-son by storm. Ord, who led the charge, was shot in the leg and had to leave the field. Bir-ney drove back the foe on the New-mar-ket road. Lee tried to make up

GRANT AND SHER-MAN AT THE CAMP FIRE.

his loss, but in vain. Fresh ground was won by the boys in blue, and both Pet-ers-burg and Rich-mond would soon have to fall.

Grant rode out to the front of But-ler's lines, and then made his way to Fort Har-ri-son. There he had to get off his horse to cross the ditch, and was soon in-side the works. The ground was strewn with blood and shells. Dead men were all round. Shells were thrown from the forts near, that burst in-side the walls. Grant stood up on the bank —the place where the men stand to fire the big guns—and had a good view of the out-works and out-guards at Rich-mond. Through the smoke the whole line could be seen for miles, and he at once made up his mind to push both

A SIG-NAL STA-TION IN A TREE.

wings of But-ler's corps to the front. He sat down to write the note. While he wrote a shell burst in the air right o'er his head. Quick as a flash the men near him bent their heads so they would not be hit. Grant did not look up; his hand did not shake; but he went on and wrote his note, and was as calm as if he had been in camp.

GEN-ER-AL GRANT AT FORT HAR-RI SON

But I set out to tell you more of Sher-i-dan, whom we left in Vir-gin-i-a. On the 13th of Oc-to-ber he was sent for to come to Wash-ing-ton, that the chiefs there might have a talk with him. He set out on the 15th and the whole force of horse-men with him as far as Front Roy-al. There, on Mon-day, the 16th, he was met by word from Wright, who had been left at Ce-dar Creek, that a note had been seized on its way to Ear-ly, which read thus: "Move as soon as my troops join you, and we will crush Sher-i-dan. — LONG-STREET.

Both Grant and Sher-i-dan had thought that Long-street was at Rich-mond, and that the Rebs had no force but Ear-ly's in that part of Vir-gin-i-a.

Sher-i-dan sent word to Wright that the horse-men would all be sent back to him, and that he must do all he could to add to his strength. "Close in on Gen-er-al Pow-ell, who will be at this point. Look well to your ground, and I know you will win." He then went on to Wash-ing-ton.

Ce-dar Creek winds its way to the North Fork of the Shen-an-do-ah, two miles east of Stras-burg. The boys in blue were in a strong place on the east bank of the creek and north of the Fork. The boys in gray were at Fish-er's Hill, five miles off. Pow-ell was at the point where the South Fork joins with the Shen-an-do-ah, more than six miles from the left of Wright's corps.

Ear-ly had a look-out on Mas-a-nut-ten mount, from which he could see the camps of all the boys in blue, and each move the troops might make. His plan was to turn Wright's left flank, as he saw that was the weak point. On the night of the 18th of Oc-to-ber, three corps of troops moved round the North Fork to the rear of Wright's force. Ker-shaw was to strike the left flank. Whar-ton to come up in front with the big guns on wheels, and charge on Wright as soon as he turned on Gor-don and Ker-shaw. Ros-ser was sent to the right flank, and Lo-max was to pass by Front Roy-al, cross the Shen-an-do-ah, and seize the road to Win-ches-ter.

The night was dark, and there was a thick fog, so that Gor-don crept past the guns of Crook and was not seen, and ere day-break had struck the rear of Wright's troops. At the same time Ker-shaw struck the left, drove in the out-posts, and bore in on the camps. Then Whar-ton came up on the front with his great guns, and the whole of the left flank gave way at the fierce fire.

The Sixth corps, on the right, had time to form and move out of camp to a ridge west of the main road, where they did their best to drive back the foe. But the big guns were brought up by the Rebs, and Get-ty fell back to the north of Mid-dle-town.

Cus-ter and Mer-ritt were sent to the left of the line to guard the road to Win-ches-ter—which Lo-max did not seize—and the rest of the boys in blue were told to fly with all haste to the rear, and they came to a halt more than six miles from the place where they had been at day-break.

Where was Sher-i-dan?

WAG-ON TRAIN UN-DER FIRE.

I told you he was on his way to Wash-ing-ton. He left there at noon, on the 18th, and that night slept at Win-ches-ter — twen-ty miles from his men. At nine o'clock the next day he rode out of Win-ches-ter. His mind was calm. He had heard no bad news. All at once he gave a start at the sounds that met his ear. He knew too well what they meant. Half a mile from the town he saw a sight that set his blood on fire. There were the boys in blue—trains and men—in a wild flight.

"Halt! Halt!"—he cries. The sight of him puts new life in the men. He rides in hot haste, swings his hat and shouts, "Turn back! turn back! turn back!" and some of the men face round at once. They will go where he leads, and do as he says, so great is the force of his will.

It was ten o'clock when Sher-i-dan got to the front,

and as soon as he saw how things were, he made his mind to fight on Get-ty's line. So he sent Cus-ter back to the right, brought up what was left of the Sixth corps, which was two miles to the right and rear, and sent word to have the 19th come up in line.

But he could not wait. There was need of haste, for the Rebs would soon make a fresh charge. So he went back him-self to urge the men on. He wore the full

SHER-I-DAN AT CE DAR CREEK.

suit of a Ma-jor Gen-er-al—which was the rank he held —and rode a fine black horse. Off he goes with a dash! Dust and foam are on man and beast. He waves his hat and sword by turns and shouts to the men to turn back. "If I had been there that would not have been!" They know it, they feel it. There is a charm in the man, a spell in his voice; he moves them; he sways them. In crowds they turn back—fall in-to ranks and are a wild mob no more.

Wright now came back to his corps, Get-ty to his—(Rick-etts had had a wound and Get-ty took his place)—and Sher-i-dan had charge of all. He formed the troops in a close line, and had a breast-work of rails and logs thrown up just in time.

The Rebs came up, but were made to fall back. They had not thought to meet such a strong force of the boys in blue. They knew they had put them to rout in fine style, but they did not know that the most of those who fled to the rear in great fright, came back and fought as if they did not know what fear was. Those who had got as far as New-town, ten miles off, came back and took part in the fight.

Sher-i-dan made an at-tack at three p.m. The Rebs fought well—back of a stone fence or a breast-work of rails—and for a while made out to check the boys in blue. But Sher-i-dan soon pushed on, and at last Ear-ly had to give way. The brave Cus-ter came up, and at his charge the whole line of troops pressed on and drove the Rebs to the creek. They could not be held back.

Night came on and hid them from sight. Ear-ly fled as far as New-mar-ket, and the whole land 'twixt the Po-to-mac and the James was in the hands of the North.

On the night of Oc-to-ber 19th, 1864, the staff were in front of Grant's tent. They had heard there had been a fight at Ce-dar Creek, and were in wait for more news. A note from Sher-i-dan was brought to Grant. He took it and read it with great care. The eyes of all the staff were on him, but his calm face gave no sign that the news was good or bad. He turned to the first page and read it to them. With a shake of the head he read of the at-tack on Wright, of the loss of guns, and how the troops had been thrown out of line and sent six miles to the rear. Here Grant made a pause, looked round at the men, and said, with a sad voice, "*That's pret-ty bad, isn't it?*"

MOS-BY'S GUER-RIL-LAS.

"It's too bad—too bad," said the men, who were quite cast down by the news.

"Now wait till I read you the rest of it," said Grant, —with a gleam of mirth in his eye. Then he went on to read how Sher-i-dan rode twen-ty miles at break-neck speed, took back the guns, won back all and more than had been lost, and left the foe a wreck.

By this time the men were wild with joy, and it was great fun for Grant to see the change that took place when he threw this bomb-shell in on them.

CHAPTER XIV.

THE FIGHT AT FIVE FORKS.

Grant's plan, as I have told you, was to "wipe out Lee;" but he did not want to move on to Rich-mond till he had the coil so tight that there would be no chance for the Rebs to break through. The hour drew near. The troops must be brought up from north, south, east, and west.

It was in Jan-u-a-ry, 1865, that Sher-man set out with his troops to march to the north by land, and to form his camp on the rail-road 'twixt Sa-van-nah and Charles-ton. Sher-man made the Rebs think he meant to move on Charles-ton or Au-gus-ta.

On the 1st of Feb-ru-a-ry he had 60,000 men in line. How-ard led the right wing. Slo-cum the left. Kil-pat-rick was chief of the horse-men.

Scho-field had charge of the force in North Car-o-li-na, and was to act with Sher-man. Thom-as was to send Gen-er-al Stone-man, with a band of horse-men, on a raid through South Car-o-li-na, well down to Co-lum-bi-a, to tear up the rail-roads there, and make a tour of that part of the State which Sher-man could not reach.

Grant, like a watch-dog, kept his eye on Lee, and would pitch in if there were signs that Lee would leave Rich-mond. "In the mean-time," said he to Sher-man, "should you be brought to a halt I can send two corps of good men to your aid from the works round Rich-mond."

Grant got word in due time of the fall of Branch-ville then of Co-lum-bi-a, then of Charles-ton. Then came word from Scho-field that Fort An-der-son and Wil-ming-ton were in his hands.

The Stars and Stripes were at the fore on the At-lan-tic and on the Gulf of Mex-i-co. Sher-i-dan, Sher-man, Scho-field, Stone-man and Meade were to close in at the same time and seize the game. Sher-i-dan set out from Win-ches-ter on the 27th of Feb-ru-ary. The spring thaws had set in, and there was great fall of rain. All the streams were too high to ford, and the march was, of course, a slow one.

On the third day he fell in with the Rebs 'twixt Har-ri-son-burg and Mount Craw-ford, and drove them back to Kline's mills.

Ear-ly was at Staun-ton, and as Sher-i-dan drew near that place the foe went on in haste to Waynes-bo-ro, where he took his stand. Cus-ter came up at once, made a dash on the breast-works and through the town, nor did he and his troops stop till they crossed the South Fork of the Shen-an-do-ah, where they stood with drawn swords and held the east bank of the stream.

The whole of Ear-ly's force threw down their arms; but Ear-ly and a few of his staff ran off, and hid in the woods till night came on. This fight took place on the 2nd of March. On the 19th, Sher-i-dan was at White House, where he found word from Grant to start at once and strike the South-side road as near to Pe-ters-burg as he could—tear it up so that it could not be built up in two or three days—and then push on to the Dan-ville road, as near Ap-po-mat-tox as he could get.

This he wrote to Sher-man; and said, "When Sher-i-dan starts I shall move out by my left with all the force I can. If Lee comes out of his lines I will do my best to beat him back."

On the 15th of March, Sher-man's left, led by Slo-cum, came up with Har-dee's force, and there was a hard fight at A-ve-rys-bo-ro, which was won by the boys in blue. Then there was a three-days' fight at Ben-tons-ville; but though Johns-ton brought to his aid such men as Bragg, Cheat-ham, Har-dee, Hamp-ton, and a large force of troops, the boys in blue held their ground, and drove the Rebs for two miles. As the road was now clear, Sher-man went on to Golds-bor-o, and there found Scho-field and his troops, who had fought their way from the heart of Ten-nes-see to the At-lan-tic. The whole of the sea-coast, and all the dock-yards, forts, and gun-boats, were now in the hands of the North, and the troops fixed so that they could take part in Grant's plan, and be near at hand when he should need them.

Sher-man's men had had a long march, and were in need of rest, so no move was made by them till the 10th of A-pril. Then they set out to cross the Ro-an-oake, and strike the Dan-ville road, which Grant thought would bring Lee out of his strong-hold. Ere the dawn of day, on the 25th of March, Lee made an at-tack on the right of Meade's line, in front of the Ninth corps, where there was a small fort, not much more than half a mile from the Ap-po-mat-tox, on the Prince George Court-house road. It was known as Fort Stead-man. From time to time some of Lee's troops had left him, and come in-to Grant's lines, and Grant had sent word to the out-guards to let all such pass and bring their arms with them. Lee knew this, and sent out a squad of men who told the out-guards that they meant to fight for the North and not for the South, and by this trick got in-side the lines, and made way for Lee's troops. The trench-guard fought hard to keep them back, but the rush was too great, and the main line gave way. In front, on the flank, and in the rear, the Rebs charged on Fort Stead-man, and the force there had not strength to hold it. It was still so dark that one could scarce see which was friend and which was foe, and this made it hard to form the troops so as to check the foe, who seized the men and turned the guns on the boys in blue.

Parke, whose line was on the east of Fort Stead-man made up his mind to re-take the fort brought up his big guns on the hills at the rear, and soon drove back the Rebs, who were on the march to the rail-road. Hartranft brought up his men to aid Parke. They were raw troops. It was the first fight they had been in, but they went to work with a will, and the cross-fire of small guns and big ones was so great that the Rebs, who were in the fort, could not get out, and so fell in the hands of the blue-coats, who took back the prize. Not a gun nor a flag was lost.

When Meade came on the field he at once sent word to Wright and Humph-reys to move west of Parke, and find out where Lee's troops were. This they did, seized a large force of men, and drove back the lines in front of their own.

All Grant's troops were to move on the 29th of March to force out Lee. On the 28th Grant sent word to Sher-i-dan to move as soon as he could in the rear of the Fifth corps, pass by its left, near to or through Din-wid-die, to reach the right and rear of Lee's troops. "Should he come out and at-tack us, or get where we can at-tack him, move in with your whole force in your own way, and feel sure that the troops will help when and where they can. I will be on the field, and will no doubt have a chance to speak with you. I mean to end the war here."

At nine o'clock Grant and his staff left Cit-y Point by

the rail-road. Lin-coln went with them to the train to bid them God-speed. "Good-bye," he said, "God bless you all!"

At dark Sher-i-dan was at Din-wid-die Court-house. Grant sent word to him—"We are now one line from the Ap-po-mat-tox to Din-wid-die. I do not want you to cut loose just now. Push round the foe if you can, and get on to his right rear. *We will all act as one* till it is seen what can be done with the Rebs."

That night the rain fell so hard that the ground was soon like a great swamp. No wheels could move through the soft mass, and men and beasts were stuck in the mud, or, what is worse, in the quick-sands. Some of the men near Grant tried hard to get him to turn back. But this he would not do. He had made up his mind, in spite of rain or roads, to push on to Rich-mond.

Some one said that Johns-ton might march up from the south and strike the blue-coats in the rear.

"I wish he would," said Grant. "I'd turn round and get rid of him and then be free to at-tack Lee."

All was gloom till Sher-i-dan rode up full of cheer to talk with Grant. Grant was in his tent, and Sher-i-dan stood out-side, by the camp-fire, with the staff. He was full of pluck, and was sure that they could beat the foe if they made the first move. He thought it was right for each man to do as the chief said, and not bring up plans of his own. His talk did much to cheer the men and Grant was sent for to hear what Sher-i-dan had to say.

There was a point near the Din-wid-die road where five roads met. It was known as the Five Forks. This was but two miles from the south-side road, and if Grant could gain Five Forks Lee could not stay in Pe-ters-burg.

Grant saw it was a good scheme, and told Sher-i-dan to go back to Din-wid-die and move at once on Five Forks.

The names of the roads that crossed here were White Oak, Din-wid-die, Boyd-ton, Vaugh-an (*vorn*), and Flat-foot.

Sher-i-dan sent out a corps from Din-wid-die Court-house, but found the Rebs in force at Five Forks. The roads were still so bad that the horse-men could not be of much use. War-ren, at the same time, made a move on the Boyd-ton road, and found the Rebs strong in his front, but was told to hold the place and do all he could to add to its strength. Wright and Parke thought it a good time to make an as-sault. Grant, who could guess the strength of Lee's force, felt that the hour had come, and at once sent word to Ord, Wright, and Parke to move on the works at day-light the next day.

Lee knew that he must hold Five Forks at all risks. Strong breast-works were put up, and all done that could be done to add to the strength of the Rebs in and round Pe-ters-burg.

On the last day of March, War-ren made a move to drive the foe from the White Oak road. The Rebs drove them back. Humph-rey sent Miles' troops to War-ren's aid, and they held the foe in check, but not till they had sent the Fifth corps a mile back, to near the Boyd-ton road.

It was all at an end by noon, and the men went to work at once to form their lines, and start off for a fresh fight. Grif-fin was to lead. Humph-rey to take from his right all the force he could spare, and with Miles, strike the foe on the left.

As soon as Meade made known this plan to Grant, he said that Humph-rey should not push to the front with-out a fair chance, and with his mind made up to go through.

At this stage of the war it would not do to fail.

So Meade made a change in his plan, and put Miles at the head of all the troops of the 2nd corps, which was to move from the left and strike on the flank all the troops in front of War-ren. This was done, and the Rebs fell back.

At one o'clock Grant went out to the front to see how the fight went on.

In the mean-time Lee had sent out Pick-ett with a strong force of men to put Sher-i-dan to rout, and on the 31st of March they were on the road to the Court-house. At the same time Sher-i-dan set out with Mer-ritt's and Crook's horse-men. Cus-ter was left at the rear to guard the roads and the trains that led to where Meade was.

For quite a space in front of the Court-house the ground is high and clear, and then slopes down to the Cham-ber-lain, a small creek on the west, the banks of which are lined with thick woods. It was here the Rebs made their first at-tack. Pick-ett and his horse-men charge—they cross the creek—but are met by so strong a foe that they have to turn back with great loss.

In the mean-time Mer-ritt had drawn near to Five Forks. It would soon have been in his hands. But a strong force of the Rebs came up and drove him back. He had to form a line west of the Five Forks road, with his rear to the Boyd-ton plank-road, and his left close to Crook's corps. Part of the Fifth corps was two and a half miles north of Din-wid-die, and would come up in time of need.

Pick-ett moved to a point on the White Oak road, struck the troops on the left of Mer-ritt, and cut off Da-vies and Mer-ritt from the main line. Sher-i-dan at once sent word to these two men to move with their troops to the Boyd-ton road, march down to Din-wid-die and join the line there.

The Rebs thought by this move that they had put the Yanks to rout, so made a left wheel and gave chase at once. This put their own rear to Sher-i-dan's main line north of Din-wid-die. Sher-i-dan was quick to see his chance, and set Gibbes and Gregg on the track of the foe.

As the Rebs went through the woods to catch Mer-ritt, they had to wheel to get on the Boyd-ton road. Gibbes struck them on flank and rear, while Gregg came up with all speed from Cham-ber-lain creek by a wood road, and came in on the left and the rear of foe. This made Pick-ett's men face the rear rank, and give up the chase for Mer-ritt, which would have brought them on the flank and rear of War-ren's troops.

Now the whole force of the Rebs, on foot and on horse, turn on the horse-men led by Sher-i-dan, and drive them back to the main line in front of Din-wid-die. Mer-ritt and Da-vies reach the Court-house too late to be of much use.

Sher-i-dan sent word to Grant that the force in his front was too strong for him. Grant at once sent troops to his aid, and not much rest did he take that night in his camp-bed at Dab-ney's saw-mill.

Lee told Pick-ett to hold Five Forks, and the Rebs ran their line out for at least two miles on the White Oak road.

Sher-i-dan had a new scheme in his mind. It was one of the tricks of war. War-ren, who led the Fifth corps, was to start out on the Five Forks road in the rear of the horse-men, turn to the right, and take a stand near the White Oak road, in front of the left flank of the foe. He was to strike the foe with his men on the left, then make a left wheel, and close in the whole flank of the foe with the rest of his corps.

Sher-i-dan next told Mer-ritt to make a move, as if he meant to turn the right of the foe, while the Fifth corps struck them on the left.

CHARGE AT FIVE FORKS.

It was late in the day when the fight took place. The Fifth corps took the lead, with Ayres on the left, Craw-ford on the right, and Grif-fin in the rear. Through mud and through brakes they tramp till they reach the broad plain. Sher-i-dan with his staff rode in the front line. Ayres' troops fell in with the Rebs ere they had got as far as the White Oak road. They were in a piece of woods, and it was hard for them to change front so as to meet the fire of the foe. The lines broke; some of the men fled to the rear, but when Sher-i-dan rode up with words of cheer most of them came back at once in-to line.

Mean-time the fire of Ayres' corps was heard by Mer-ritt, and the horse-men at once made their charge. These had to bear the brunt of the fight, as they were well to the front on the main Five Forks road. There was one point on this road that both sides fought to gain. If Ayres could get there he could rake with shot the whole length of the White Oak road.

Craw-ford and Grif-fin had got so far out of line that they could not help Ayres at all, and his troops were in a tight place. The breast-work of the Rebs was both strong and long, and hid by a dense growth of low pines.

Sher-i-dan bids the bands play. He takes the flag in his own hands, and leads the charge at the head of the line. With a rush and a sweep Ayres' troops crowd on the flank of the foe, drive them back with the points of their guns, break up their lines, and seize a large force of men.

Grif-fin, who by this time finds he is not in the right place, brings his troops up on a run, comes in on the right of Ayres in time to seize a large force of the Rebs. Craw-ford is brought round to the Ford road. His

PRIS-O-NERS CAP-TUR-ED AT FIVE FORKS.

troops face the south, and the Rebs in their flight rush, as it were, in-to the arms of the boys in blue.

Thus the works in front fell in the hands of Mer-ritt's men, who fought on foot and on horse-back, and with the aid of the rest of the force drove the Rebs back to the Forks. There they made no stand, but fled down the White Oak road. Grif-fin kept on their track till night came on, and they were then six miles from where the fight took place.

The rain had ceased but the night was dark. Grant sat out-side of his tent. Two or three of his staff stood near the camp-fire in the wet woods. Two had been with Sher-i-dan all day to bring back the news. The

GRANT WAIT-ING FOR NEWS.

cheers of the troops were heard. No need to tell what they meant. Five Forks was won!

The one who brought the good news to Grant was Col-o-nel (*Ker-nel*) Hor-ace Por-ter. He came up in such a wild state of joy, and did such queer things that some of the men thought he had had a drop too much. But he was not drunk with wine. It is said that his mate—the one who had gone with him to the front—was not a bit more calm. He had been shot in the foot at some time, and wore a steel boot on that foot. When he had the word to mount and ride to the front, he put the steel boot on the leg that was not hurt. It was not strange that such news should turn the brain.

CHAPTER XV.

ON TO RICHMOND.

WHEN Grant had heard the news from Five Forks he went in his tent, and wrote a note to Meade, to urge him to move at once lest Lee should leave Pe-ters-burg and press hard on Sher-i-dan.

"Wright and Parke should both be sent out to feel for a chance to get through Lee's line *at once*, and if they can get through should push on *to-night*."

No time to rest now. Push—push—push—was the

PUSH—PUSH—PUSH—WAS THE WORD

word sent to Sher-i-dan and Ord. "I would fix twelve to-night," he said; "but the troops could not be got in line at that hour."

The at-tack was made at dawn on the 2nd of A-pril. It is still so dark that the men can just see where to step. Not a word is said as they move on through the mud. Here and there, at the head of the line, may be seen a man with an axe to cut down the trees that screen the earth-works of the foe. The first of these out-works soon falls in the hands of Wright. The fight is sharp, but brief, and the boys in blue can-not be held in check. They reach the Boyd-ton road and the South-side rail-way, break up the rails, and cut the wires from the poles. As soon as he can, Wright forms his troops in line once more and moves down to Hatch-er's Run. Here they have a brush with the foe, whom they soon put to rout.

Parke set out by the Je-ru-sa-lem plank road, at the end of which the Rebs had a strong earth-work. A large force join Parke at this point and they push on through shot and shell, in close ranks, take the fort by storm, and turn its guns on the foe.

It was now day-light. The loss on both sides had been great. The fort was a strong one, and the Rebs fought hard to keep hold of it. But in-side of it was a long chain of works that Grant would have to take ere he could reach Pe-ters-burg. He felt sure that the rest could do as well as Parke and Wright had done.

In an hour or two word came from Ord, "We have the forts next to Hatch-er's Run on both sides."

Grant at once made up his mind to face the whole force of Meade and Ord to the east and hem in Pe-ters-burg. He rode down to the right and told his plan to Meade. Then he rode up on some high ground from whence he could look on the field of bat-tle. The point

GRANT ON THE HILL.

was less than a mile from the main line of Lee's troops, and not three miles from the heart of Pe-ters-burg. Here he got off his horse, and sat down on the ground near a farm-house to wait for the word that Meade, Sher-i-dan, or Ord might send

The Rebs turned their guns on the group, and the place was soon quite hot. Grant sat with his back to a tree, while the shot fell round him thick and fast.

His aides-de-camp, who are in dread lest he should lose his life, urge him to leave the spot. He looks up with an odd smile, and says, "Well, the Rebs do seem to have the range of this place. I guess we might as well leave," and soon Grant and his staff ride off at a quick pace, and out of harm's way.

All that day the fight was kept up, and one by one the works round Pe-ters-burg fell in the hands of Grant's men. Forts Gregg and Bald-win held out till the last. If the blue-coats take them at all, they must take them by storm. At one o'clock in the day Ord's men charge on the fort. The Rebs fight well, and more than

WAG-ON TRAIN.

once drive back the boys in blue. At last they reach the wall, and for half an hour a hand-to-hand fight is kept up; some of the men use their guns as clubs. At the end of that time the Stars and Stripes float from the top of Fort Gregg. Those in Fort Bald-win make haste to flee, but the blue-coats turn the guns of Fort Gregg on them and force them to sur-ren-der.

When night fell on the 2nd of A-pril, Lee still held the line south of the Ap-po-mat-tox. Pick-ett and Bush-rod Johns-ton were on the way to A-me-li-a Court-house. They had to cross the stream where they could find a bridge or a ford. The men were worn out. They had had a long fast. Now and then they had to halt for rest. Some were so weak that they fell by the way-side, but all were in hopes to reach A-me-li-a Court-house, and find there the food of which they were so much in need.

It was a sad night-march. There were no lines for them to hold, no earth-works for them to guard. Lee had left Pe-ters-burg!

By dawn of the next day, Grant's men were on his track; not in the rear, but to head him off.

No news had as yet come from Rich-mond. Were the Rebs there? Would they try to hold it? Grant rode out in front of Ord's line, and on the way a note was put in his hands from Weit-zel. It said, "Rich-mond is ours. The Rebs left in great haste, and set the town on fire."

Swift goes the word through the lines: "Rich-mond is ours! Rich-mond is ours!"

"Ah, is it!" say the troops; "well we must make haste to catch Lee."

Oh, what a night that was in Rich-mond! Crowds were in all the streets. Men mad with rage or rum set fire to mills, stores, and work-shops. The guards of the jails fled from their posts, and men who had been shut up for their crimes were free to rob, or burn, or do what harm they would. Shouts, yells, and cries were heard on all sides, and now and then there was a great shock from the rams and gun-boats that were blown up so that they might not fall in the hands of the North.

U-NION TROOPS EN-TER-ING RICH-MOND

Thus Rich-mond fell. A New York boy was the first to raise the Stars and Stripes, and by night mob-rule was at an end, the fires were put out, and the hush of peace came to heal the blows of sound.

Mean-while Grant had gone on with the head of Ord's line, and by six o'clock was at a point half way 'twixt Not-ta-way Court-house and Burks-ville. He gave the road to the troops, as was his wont, and rode with his staff in a piece of woods, when a man in the dress of a Reb was brought up to him. One of Grant's staff knew him at once as a scout of Sher-i-dan's. The man took from his mouth a quid of to-bac-co in which was a small pill of tin-foil. In this pill was a note from Sher-i-dan, who wrote: "Am at Je-ters-ville. Wish you were here. I see no chance for Lee to get out."

FEED-ING THE HUN-GRY.

Grant got on a fresh horse, and set out at once with a score of men, some of whom were on his staff, to meet Sher-i-dan. None but the scout knew the way. The men were not sure they could trust him. Soon night came on. The ride was long, the roads were rough, and there were dense woods to go through. Grant rode at the head of the small band, each one of whom was sworn to take care of his chief. What a prize he would be to fall in-to the hands of the foe! Sharp eyes peer to right and left. An aide-de-camp keeps a watch on the scout, who proves to be a good and true man, for at the end of a four hours' ride Grant and his staff come on Sher-i-dan's out-posts. These men doubt the truth of what is told them. It could not be that Grant—the Gen-er-al-in-chief—would ride at night, and with so few men, so close to the lines of the foe. But they find it is so, and then let them pass the guards, and haste to Sher-i-dan's camp.

CHAPTER XVI.

"LET US HAVE PEACE."

We left Lee on his way to A-me-li-a Court-house, where he was in hopes to find food, and from there make his way to Johns-ton. But when he came to A-me-li-a he found no food, and so set out at once for Lynch-burg. His men had had no food for two days. To fight by day and march by night was too much for them in their weak state, and some of those who had been the most brave threw down their arms, and left the ranks.

Still a great host press on, and reach Sail-or's creek on the 6th of A-pril. There they find Sher-i-dan in front of them. The troops halt and form in line, while the big guns and wains pass on to cross the Ap-po-mat-tox at Farm-ville.

But Grant had sent Ord to burn the bridge at Farm-ville, which was a small town north-west of Burks-ville. The South-side rail-road crossed the Ap-po-mat-tox twice near this place; first at High Bridge, five miles east of the town, and then at Farm-ville. And you had-

THE BURN-ING BRIDGE

to cross the Ap-po-mat-tox in the town to get on the road to Lynch-burg.

The stream was too deep to ford, and blue-coats and gray-coats head at once for Farm-ville.

Ord had sent Gen-er-al The-o-dore Read, his chief of staff, to lead the horse-men to High Bridge, which they were to burn. But on the way they fell in with Lee's troop of horse, and the two bands had a fierce fight. Read got his death-wound—so did Wash-burne—and at last there was no one to lead the men, and they had to give up and hand their swords to the foe. The hard fight at this point made Lee think that a large force of blue-coats had struck the head of his line, so he had this part of his troops halt, and throw up earth-works, and make the place as strong as they could.

This gave Sher-i-dan time to come up with Lee's men who were on the Dea-tons-ville road.

Grant staid in Je-ters-ville, to be as near as he could to all the lines of his troops which were sent out from that point. From a hill-top he could see all that took place on both sides.

Crook was sent to flank the train at Dea-tons-ville. Mer-ritt was to pass to the left, and both were to press in on the foe till they struck a weak point. Stagg led a troop of horse-men and made a charge on Lee's lines, while Mil-ler's big guns, from a crest at the rear sent shells in the breast-works of the foe, and set fire to the trains.

Then the Sixth corps came up and Wright drove the Rebs for two miles, through a thick swamp, and back as far as Sail-or's creek. They were shut in on all sides. There was nought to do but yield. From the hill-sides in the rear Mer-ritt and Crook with their brave horse-men, swept through the pine-trees like a whirl-wind. The Rebs fought hard on all sides, and at last threw down their arms, and brought the fight to a close.

At dawn on the 7th of A-pril, Ord found that the Rebs had left his front, and were on their way to Farm-ville. He at once put his troops in line of march and came up on Lee's flank and rear just as he got in-to the town. So Lee had no chance to stop, but sent the wains by rail to Ap-po-mat-tox, while he and his troops took the road on the north bank.

But Grant was at his heels. Ere day-light Sher-i-dan had set out from Sail-or's creek, and was soon on the road to Prince Edward.

Humph-reys came up with the rear of the foe at High Bridge, which he found had been set on fire. The gray-coats tried to hold it till it was quite burnt up, but at last were put to flight, and the rail-road bridge was saved with the loss of but four spans.

Sharp fights took place here and there on the road, for when gray met blue there was sure to be a flash of fire. More than once the boys in gray, though well spent, drove back the boys in blue from some point they had set out to gain. At night the Rebs had been chased for miles on the banks of the Ap-po-mat-tox, and were made to cross the stream in such haste that they had no chance to more than half burn the bridge, and had to leave quite a lot of their big guns.

The van-guard of both Humph-reys and Crook came up with the Rebs north of the stream. At the south, Sher-i-dan, with Grif-fin and Ord, spread out his troops on both sides, like two great wings, to check Lee's flight. Lynch-burg was Lee's last hope.

In the last days of March, Stone-man had set out from east Ten-nes-see, and was at this time on his way to the rail-road west of Lynch-burg. He was not quite to the town, but was so near that there was no chance for Lee to get out of the net in which he was caught.

On the night of the 7th of April, Grant came to Farm-ville, and slept at the same inn where Lee had slept on the night of the 6th. All night long the Sixth corps went through Farm-ville on the track of Lee. Camp fires were in the streets, and out on the hills and fields. The folks who dwelt in this small town were in a great state of fright. War had come right to their doors. The noise, the glare, the flash of arms, were sights and sounds quite new to them.

Grant came out on the porch of the inn to see the Sixth Corps march by. The night was quite dark, but the camp fires threw their gleams on his face, and the troops saw it was their chief who stood there. Their shouts rang through the air.

Grant stood still till the last of the troops went by then went in and wrote a note to Robert E. Lee. He told him that it was his wish to shed no more blood, and that Lee must see that it was best for the South to end the strife here and now.

Lee's own men—those who had the right to speak to him in this way—had urged him to sur-ren-der. But he

THE FLAG OF TRUCE.

could not bear to do it. "The time is not yet come," he said. But he wrote to Grant, to say that he did not think he was in such a strait as Grant made out, and to ask what the terms would be if he made up his mind to end the strife, and give up his sword.

This note came to Grant on the eighth of A-pril, while he was still at Farm-ville, and he at once sent back word to Lee that his one great wish was for peace. The terms were that the whole ar-my of North-ern Vir-gin-i-a should lay down their arms, and serve the Stars and Stripes.

In the mean-time the Rebs kept up their flight, with Grant's men in hot chase. Grant set out to join Sher-i-dan. Worn out with loss of sleep, and the weight of care that was on his mind, he fell ill and had to halt at a farm-house on the road, where he spent most of the day.

CA-VAL-RY PUR-SU-ING GEN-ER-AL LEE'S AR-MY.

Near mid-night, while still in great pain, a note came to him from Lee, who said that he did not think the time had come for him to lay down his arms, but as peace should be the aim of all, it was his wish to know if Grant's terms would lead to that end. That he would meet him at 10 a.m., the next day, on the old stage-road to Rich-mond, not to sur-ren-der the whole ar-my, but to find out his terms for the force that he had led out of Rich-mond and that were still slaves of his will.

This note was not quite as frank as the first one had been. Grant wrote back that his wish was for peace. "*The terms on which peace can be had are well un-der-stood.* Let the South lay down their arms. This would save life, and bring the war at once to an end."

He then set out to join Sher-i-dan, and speed that which he knew must soon come to pass. For when a man asks for terms it is a sign that he is weak, and cannot hold out.

Ord's men marched from day-light on the 8th, to day-light on the 9th. Grif-fin did as well as Ord. The troops found no fault.

"Theirs but to *do* and *die*."

Lee's troops soon came up to where Sher-i-dan stood in wait for them. They must make their way through now, or all is lost. Lee's troops are on foot. There are far more of them than Sher-i-dan has, and they make one bold push for the goal they hope to reach. They give the well-known yell. They start on a run. More fierce is the fire of their guns. Sher-i-dan's horse-men fall back. Lee's troops pass on? No. It was but a ruse, a trick on the part of the boys in blue. Out of the woods, down from the hill-sides, in front, in rear, on the right, and on the left, the blue-coats come, and close in round the poor boys in gray. It is their hour of doom.

Sher-i-dan was on their left. The word "charge!" was on his lips, when lo! a white flag was seen. The man who bore it came from Lee, who was at Ap-po-mat-tox Court-house. Sher-i-dan rode at once to the Court-house and there met Gen-er-als Gor-don and Wil-cox, who told him that Lee had sent to Grant for terms of peace. He thought it strange, if this were so, that Lee should make the at-taek on his lines. If he had sent to Grant he had no right to fight Sher-i-dan. But Gor-don said it was true, that Lee had made up his mind to yield, and strife must cease till word came from Grant.

Lee's note of the 9th of A-pril did not reach Grant till near noon. In it he said he would meet Grant on his own terms. Grant had left the Rich-mond and Lynch-burg roads, and was on the Farm-ville and Lynch-burg road—four miles west of Walk-er's church. He wrote to Lee that he would push to the front to meet him at the place Lee might choose.

STACK-ING ARMS.

This note from Grant was put in the hands of Col-o-nel Bab-cock, one of his staff, who at once set forth with it, rode past the out-guards

of the foe, and was led by one of Lee's men up to the great chief.

He and his staff sat by the road-side in the shade of a large tree, but as soon as Lee read the note he sprang on his horse and set out to find a place where he and Grant could meet and fix the terms of peace. He rode as far as the small town of Ap-po-mat-tox, and made choice of a house where dwelt a man by the name of McLean.

The troops in blue and gray were drawn up at the foot of a ridge, on each side of Ap-po-mat-tox which was on a knoll, and could be seen for miles. The McLean house was a plain farm-house, with a porch in front. The two chiefs met, shook hands, and then went in the small room at the side of the hall. Some of Grant's staff went with them.

ON THE WAY HOME.

Lee was in full dress, and wore at his side a fine sword, the gift, it was said, of the State of Vir-gin-i-a, while Grant, and those who were with him, were in plain clothes—full of stains, and much worn. Some of them had slept in their boots for days, and Grant did not have his sword with him. One of the men made bold to ask

THE MARCH ON PENN-SYL-VA-NI-A AV-E-NUE.

Mar-shall (Lee's aide-de-camp) how it came that he and his chief were dressed up so fine, and he said that when Sher-i-dan came on them they found they had time to save but one suit of clothes, so each man took the best he had.

Lee told Grant that he had sent for him that he might know on what terms peace could be had. Grant made no change in the terms, and Lee must have known that

he would not. "Write them out," he said to Grant, "and I will sign them."

So Grant sat down to write them out, and as he wrote he gave a glance at Lee and saw the bright sword that was at his side. That made him change his mind. Lee and his staff were brave men. They had fought well. Grant knew how it must hurt their pride to bend their knees to him. He would be as kind as he could. They should keep their swords.

The terms were drawn up. Lee signed them. The two chiefs shook hands, and then rode off. As Lee rides down his lines the men rush up in crowds to their chief. Each one strives to touch his hand. Tears stream down his cheeks as he says to them, "I have done what I think is best for you. My heart is too full to speak, but I wish you all health and joy."

GRANT AT THE RE-VIEW-ING STAND.

So the war was at an end. When it first broke out it was thought that it would not last more than a few months, but it had gone on for four long years, and had cost oh! more than words or tongue can tell. And oh, how sweet it was to be at peace once more! No North, no South, but one great na-tion; and one flag—the same old flag—to wave o'er us all!

CHAPTER XVII.

THE LAST FIGHT OF ALL.

THERE was one way in which we could pay in part the debt which we owed to Grant. This was to make him chief of the land, in Lin-coln's place. It was on the 9th of A-pril, 1865, that Grant and Lee met at Ap-po-mat-tox Court-house. Five days from that time Lin-coln was shot, at a play-house, by J. Wilkes Booth. An-drew John-son had to act as chief till his term was out. Then Grant took his place. The North votes for him as one man. There is no one so great as he.

With U. S. Grant at the helm there will be peace for *us*, and for the whole U-ni-ted States.

Grant serves for eight years, and at the end of that time goes back to the home-life and the home-ways of which he is so fond.

He has made hosts of friends through-out the length and breadth of the land.

A score of years goes by, and then comes sad news. A foe draws near that Grant can-not bring to terms. The name of this foe is Death. Pain is his aide-de-camp.

For long days and weeks the strife goes on. Then hope springs up. There is a chance that he may live for some years yet. But it is a false hope. The bright flash of a flame that ere long will go out.

Grant is calm and brave. He has a strong will. There is some work he must do for those he loves. So in spite of pain, and the loss of sleep, he writes the book that tells of his own life. Kind friends—the best of care—and his own strong will—keep death at bay. All is done that can be done to ease his pain.

Late in the Spring of 1885 the sick man is borne out of New York, and up to Mount Mac-greg-or—near Sar-a-to-ga—where the air is pure and fresh, and there is no noise to jar on the nerves.

Here the strife goes on. As the warm days come on he sits out on the porch, and lists to the songs of the birds, and the voice of the wind through the trees.

What a strange life for one who led troops to war, and went through blood, fire, and smoke to save the land, and the flag so dear to him! At the end of eight months of pain, that but few brave men could have borne so well, peace comes to Gen-er-al Grant. No more strife, no more pain, no more heart-ache for him. He is at rest.

Great grief is felt all through the land. The streets of all the great towns are draped with black.

Crowds go to see where the dead man lies in state. For three days they pass in a line—at times eight blocks long—that has no break till night sets in, and the doors are shut. Rich and poor join hands. North and South are one in this sad hour.

Grant died on the 8th of Ju-ly. The last sad rites took place on the 8th of Au-gust. Those who had been his foes when the North and South were at war, met as one, and took part in the march to the tomb, where the great man was to be laid. No such sight had been seen in New York. It was as if a king were borne through the streets; but few kings could have had such a hold on men's hearts.

Grant won a great name, and great fame; but that which gave him the most joy was that he had, by God's help, brought peace to those who were at strife.

U-lys-ses S. Grant was great in his life, and great in his death; and for years to come men from all parts of the world will flock to his tomb and tell of the great deeds he did, and the way in which he wound up the war.

The key-note of his life was "do right and fear not;" and from his grave he seems to say to one and all

"LET US HAVE PEACE."

Made in United States
Orlando, FL
21 February 2022

15030747R00111